HighTide
In collaboration with
the National Theatre
and the Bush Theatre
presents

stovepipe

a new play by Adam Brace

First performance as part of HighTide
Festival 2008, The Cut, Halesworth,
Suffolk on 1 May 2008.

London opening on
3 March 2009 at
The West 12 Centre,
Shepherds Bush,
London.

**National
Theatre**

bush theatre

Cast

Stovepipe

a new play by Adam Brace

ANDRE / GRIF
CHRISTIAN BRADLEY

ALAN
SHAUN DOOLEY

EDDY / HARRY
NIALL MACGREGOR

CAROLYN / MASHA / SALLY
ELEANOR MATSUURA

SAAD / MARTY / RAMI
SARGON YELDA

Director: **Michael Longhurst**
Producers: **Samuel Hodges &**
Steven Jon Atkinson
Dramaturgy: **Jack Bradley**
Design: **takis**
Lighting: **Matt Prentice**
Sound: **Steve Mayo**

Voice: **John Tucker**
Casting: **Joyce Nettles**
Assistant Director: **Titas Halder**
Fight Choreography: **Rachel Bown-Williams**
Production Manager: **Richard Eustace**
Stage Manager: **Jonathan Goldstone**
Deputy Stage Manager: **Jennifer Simpson**
Assistant Stage Manager: **Naomi Brooks**
Front of House Manager: **Lucinda Springett**
Production Electrician: **Robert Stemson**

Construction: **Nick Hardwick**
Construction Assistant: **Jack Brooks**
Associate Sound Designer: **Luke Swaffield**
Sound Secondment: **Gemma Harrison**
Photography: **Sophie Vickers**
Press Representation: **David Bloom at Target**
Live. 020 7907 1777.

HighTide wishes to thank Sebastian Born, Nicholas Hytner, Nick Starr, Tom Morris, Sarah Hunt, Sarah Chambers, Michael Straughan, Rich Walsh, Ben Vernon and others at the National Theatre; Josie Rourke, Angela Bond, Caroline Dyott, Sam Craven-Griffiths, Tara Wilkinson, Ewan Thomson, Alix Hearn, Clare Moss and others at the Bush Theatre; Jason King and others at West 12; Marvin Patel and Fitness First, Shepherd's Bush; Thelma Holt, Malcolm Taylor, Nick Salmon and Natasha Ockrent at Stage One; Richard Lee and The Jerwood Space; John Aston and Philips; Barbican International Theatre Events; Ian Dickinson and Dave Mcseveney at The Royal Court Theatre; Gary Giles and Dave Gregory at Cue One; Richard Nowlles at Richard Nowells Sound Services; Phil Hurley at Stage Sound Services; Tony Illman; Chris Ryan and Caroline Hall; Sue Emmas; David Lan; Syreeta Woolton; Sarah Cleave; Lyndsey Turner; Ali Khalid Laith; Tara Wilkinson; Davina Shah, Toby Knowles, The IMarEST for their support on the London transfer of this production.

The London transfer of *Stovepipe* is generously supported by the Theatre Investment Fund / Society of London Theatre Award for New Producers.

Design Team Credits:

Katerina Angelopoulou, Clare Amos, Lily Arnold, Carla Cuomo, Stephanie Baguet, Julia Drummond-Haig, Emma Habbeshon, Gwenllian Hylton, Cassandra Jackson, Electra Kythreotou, Georgia Lowe, Pablo Marks, Rosie Mclaren, Rachel Morgan, George Moustakas, James Penzer, Helen Quinn-Gregson, Eugenia Sanchez, Andrea Santamarina, Richard Scattergood, Rachel E. Stanners, Leyla Weller, Yaara Zadok, Andrew Grange, Joshua Carr, John Gilroy, Samantha Marshall.

Cast

CHRISTIAN BRADLEY
Trained at RADA
* For HighTide: *Stovepipe* (HighTide Festival 2008).
* Other theatre includes: *Our Friends in The North* (Northern Stage); *Macbeth* (West Yorkshire Playhouse); *Paradise Lost* (Headlong); *The Seduction of God* (The Wrestling School); *The Romans In Britain* (Crucible Sheffield); *Scapino The Trickster* (Purcarete/Chichester); *5/11* (Chichester); *Antigone* (Cheek by Jowl/Old Vic); *Merlin* (Library Manchester); *Mariana Pineda* (The Gate); *Peer Gynt* (Southwark Playhouse); The Stoning (BAC); *The Disputation* (Hampstead); *Schweyk* (Copeau Festival, France).
* Television includes: *Merlin*.
* Film includes: *Rugby Road, Tainted Heart, Finishing School*.

SHAUN DOOLEY
* For HighTide: *Stovepipe* (HighTide Festival 2008).
* Other theatre includes: *Brassed Off* (Sheffield Crucible and Royal National Theatre); *The White Devil* (Lyric Hammersmith); *Summer Begins* (Southwark Playhouse); *Kiss of the Spiderwoman* (Nottingham Playhouse).
* Television includes: *Apparitions; Silent Witness; Midsommer Murders; Harley Street; An Accident Waiting to Happen; The Street; Vincent; Mobile; Foyle's War; Warriors; Shackleton*.
* Film includes: *Red Riding Trilogy; Kandahar Break; The Appointment; Mark of Cain; Eden Lake; Salvage*.
* Awards include: the Royal Television Society (North) Best Actor Award for the multi award-winning Mark of Cain.

NIALL MACGREGOR
Trained at Bristol Old Vic Theatre School.
* For HighTide: *Stovepipe* (HighTide Festival 2008).
* Television includes: *The Commander; Messiah; To The Ends Of The Earth; Warriors; Dalziel & Pascoe; Rough Crossings; Party Animals; Low Winter Sun; Holby City; Monarch of the Glen; Silent Witness; The Bill*.
* Film includes: *The Flying Scotsman*.
* Radio includes: Voices from the Front Line.

ELEANOR MATSUURA
Trained at The Central School of Speech and Drama.
* For HighTide: *Stovepipe* (HighTide Festival 2008) and *Assembly* (Hay-on-Wye Festival 2008).
* Other theatre includes: *Love Is Just a Possibility* (Royal Court); Novel and 24 Hour Plays: *Revolution* (Old Vic); *Coriolanus* (RSC).
* Television includes: *Hunter; The Old Guys; FM; Lead Balloon; Dr Who; Casualty; My Family; Trial and Retribution; After You've Gone; EastEnders; A Very Social Secretary; Green Wing; Extras; Hustle*.
* Film includes: *Magicians; After The Rain; Breaking and Entering*.

SARGON YELDA
* For HighTide: *Stovepipe* (HighTide Festival 2008).
* Television includes: *Saddam's Tribe; Midnight Man; Compulsion*.

Company

ADAM BRACE (WRITER)
Adam was born in London in 1980. He studied Writing for Performance (MA) at Goldsmiths and is Dramaturg with the company Simple8.
* For HighTide: *Stovepipe* (HighTide Festival 2008.
* As Writer/Director: *Because It's There* (Underbelly, Theatre 503).
* As Writer: *A Real Humane Person Who Cares and All That*, *The Strange Case of Dr Jekyll and Mr Hyde* (both Edinburgh Fringe).

STEVEN JON ATKINSON (PRODUCER)
* For HighTide: as Director - *Muhmah* (Aldeburgh Music); *The Pitch* (Latitude Festival 2008); as Producer; *I Caught Crabs in Walberswick* (HighTide Festival 2008 & Edinburgh Festival & Bush Theatre); *Switzerland* (HighTide Festival 2008); *Certain Dark Things* (HighTide Festival 2008 & BAC); *Stovepipe* (HighTide Festival 2008).
* Other directing includes: *Freedom Trilogy* (Hull Truck); *Sexual Perversity in Chicago* (Edinburgh).
* Awards include: SOLT Stage One Bursary for New Producers.
Steven is Artistic Director of HighTide. Previously he was Literary Manager of Hull Truck Theatre and an assistant director at Shakespeare's Globe.

RACHEL BOWN-WILLIAMS (FIGHT CHOREOGRAPHER)
Rachel is co founder and director of Rc-Annie Fight Company, which specialises in fight choreography and training for the Entertainment Industry. She has taught Stage Combat at Drama Centre, Central School Of Speech and Drama, Arts Ed, East 15, LIPA and Cygnet Training Company.
* Fight Choreographing experience includes: *Stovepipe* (HighTide Festival 2008), *A Chorus of Disapproval* (Clwyd Theatr Cymru), *Cargo* (Oval House Theatre), *Woyzeck* (Cardboard Citizens), *Lundon* (Uzong Films and Entertainment), *The Hunt for Gollum* (Residue Movies) and *Gracie* (24 FIlms).
Rachel was part of the Motion Capture team on *Poseidon* for Warner Bros.

JACK BRADLEY (DRAMATURG)
* For HighTide: *Stovepipe* (HighTide Festival 2008).
Currently Literary Associate to Sonia Friedman Productions in the West End of London, Associate of the Tricycle Theatre, and advisor to the Scottish Arts Council. Previously he was Literary Manager of Soho Theatre (1989-94) and Literary Manager of the Royal National Theatre for twelve years, advising on the repertoire for Richard Eyre, Trevor Nunn and Nicholas Hytner, spearheading their new play policy.
Jack is an Artistic Advisor of HighTide.

TITAS HALDER (ASSISTANT DIRECTOR)
Titas is Literary Associate at the Finborough Theatre. He was a participant of the Young Vic Summer School 2008.
* Directing includes: *One for the Road* (Tabard).
* Assistant Directing includes: *Follow, Sons of York* (Finborough); *The Constant Prince* (Oxford Playhouse).
* Writing includes: *Feeding Me* (Paines Plough Later); *Fresh Prince* (Oval House 33% London.

SAMUEL HODGES (PRODUCER)
* For HighTide: as Actor - *Assembly/Lyre* (HighTide Festival 2007); as Producer - *I Caught Crabs in Walberswick* (HighTide Festival 2008 & Edinburgh Festival & Bush Theatre); *Switzerland* (HighTide Festival 2008); *Certain Dark Things* (HighTide Festival 2008 & BAC); *Stovepipe* (HighTide Festival 2008); *Assembly* (HighTide Festival 2007 & Hay-on-Wye Festival 2008); *Weightless, You Were After Poetry, Lyre, and Ned & Sharon* (HighTide Festival 2008).
* Other theatre includes: *The Winslow Boy* (Salisbury Playhouse); *A Man for All Seasons* (York Theatre Royal); *Men Without Shadows* (Finborough Theatre); *Anatol* (Arcola Theatre); *The Fall of the House of Usher* (Etcetera Theatre and Cambridge Playrooms).
* Television includes: *Broadside; Doctors; Cambridge Spies.*
* Film includes: *Player* (writer, actor and producer).
* Awards include: SOLT Stage One Bursary for New Producers 2008, Best Short Film Nominations at Raindance and Miami Film Festivals (*Player*).
Samuel is the founder and Artistic Director of HighTide.

MICHAEL LONGHURST (DIRECTOR):

Training: Mountview Postgraduate Directing Course.

* For HighTide: The Contingency Plan: On the Beach (Bush Theatre, forthcoming), *Stovepipe* (HighTide Festival 2008).
* As Director: *dirty butterfly* (Young Vic); *One in Five* (Daring Pairings Festival, Hampstead Theatre); *Gaudeamus* (Arcola); *New Voices: The 24 Hour Plays 2006* (Old Vic); *Guardians* (Edinburgh Pleasance & Theatre503); *Cargo* (Edinburgh Pleasance & Oval House Theatre); *Doctor Faustus* (Djanogly Lakeside Theatre, Nottingham). Michael has worked as an Assistant Director at the Young Vic, Old Vic & Royal Court.
* Awards: Jerwood Directors Award 2007; Fringe First Award 2005.

STEVE MAYO (SOUND DESIGNER)

* For HighTide: *I Caught Crabs in Walberswick* (HighTide Festival 2008 & Edinburgh Festival & Bush Theatre); *Stovepipe* (HighTide Festival 2008); *Weightless, You Were After Poetry, Lyre and Ned & Sharon* (HighTide Festival 2007).
* Other theatre includes: *Well* (Apollo Theatre); *Sh*t M*x*(Trafalgar Studios); *Fight Face* (Lyric Studio); *Lie of the Land; Lough/Rain* (Edinburgh 08); *Hangover Square* (Finborough Theatre); *Absolutely Frank* (Queen's Theatre Hornchurch); *Snowbound* (Trafalgar Studios); *Jack and the Beanstalk,* (Barbican Theatre); *Romeo and Juliet* (BAC); *Future/ Perfect* (Soho Theatre); *Eden's Empire* (Finborough Theatre); *Miniaturists* (Arcola); *Mythomania* (White Bear Theatre); *Tale of Two Cities* (G.S.M.D); *Cinderella* (G.S.M.D); *Dr Foster* (Menier Chocolate Factory); *Silence* (Arcola).
* Composition: *Simpatico* (Old Red Lion) (as Urt); *Absolutely Frank* (Queen's Theatre). Steve is Head of Sound at Barbican International Theatre Events. www.steve-mayo.co.uk

MATT PRENTICE (LIGHTING DESIGNER)

Training: Bristol Old Vic

* For HighTide: *I Caught Crabs in Walberswick* (HighTide Festival 2008 & Edinburgh Festival & Bush Theatre); *Switzerland* (HighTide Festival 2008); *Certain Dark Things* (HighTide Festival 2008); *Stovepipe* (HighTide Festival 2008).
* Other theatre includes: *Parade* (South Side Edinburgh); *A Chorus Line* (Shaw Theatre); *The House of Bernarda Alba* (The Players Theatre); *The Young People's Theatre Company Showcase* (Gielgud Theatre); *Faust* (Punch-drunk and the National Theatre); *Peter Pan* (The Assembly Room, Derby); *Masque of the Red Death* (Punch-drunk, BAC).
* Awards include: Best Production Design, Critics Circle Awards 2006 for Faust. Matt is Head of Lighting at the Royal Academy of Dramatic Art and was previously the Head of Lighting at the Mountview Academy of Theatre Arts.

takis (DESIGNER)

* For HighTide: *I Caught Crabs in Walberswick* (HighTide Festival 2008 & Edinburgh Festival & Bush Theatre); *Switzerland* (HighTide Festival 2008); *Certain Dark Things* (HighTide Festival 2008); *Stovepipe* (HighTide Festival 2008).
* Other theatre Includes: *The Marriage Bed* (Hong Kong/ NY); *Invasion* (Soho Theatre); *Boxergirl* (RADA); *A Tale for Winter* (UK tour); *Scenes from the Big Picture* (RADA); *Marat/Sade* (Jermyn Street Theatre); *Crazy Lady* (Drill Hall & Contact Theatre Manchester); *Nikolina* (Pleasance Courtyard, Edinburgh Fringe Festival); *Schweyk in the Second World War* (Duisburg); *Medea* (Greece/Italy)...
* Installations includes: *Forgotten Peacock* (Design Museum/The Brunswick), *Installation 496* (RADA), Goldfish (Paris), *Mythological Installation Oedipus* (Bucharest), *Visual Performance in Baroque Spirit* (Venice)... Music Performances includes: Maria Callas - *Vissi D'arte, Vissi D'amore* (Barbican), *Choruses* (Ancient Epidaurus/ Frankfurt), *The Words of Love* (Athens), *In the Light of the Night* (Ancient Epidaurus), *Nikos Skalkotas* (Queen Elizabeth Hall)...
* Film includes: *Eve* (European Festivals). For more information: www.takis.info

JOHN TUCKER MA (VOICE)

* For HighTide: as Associate Voice Coach: *I Caught Crabs in Walberswick* (HighTide Festival 2008 & Edinburgh Festival & Bush Theatre); *Switzerland* (HighTide Festival 2008); *Certain Dark Things* (HighTide Festival 2008 & BAC); *Stovepipe* (HighTide Festival 2008); *Lyre; Ned and Sharon; You Were After Poetry; Weightless* (HighTide Festival 2007).
* TV includes: *Classical Star* (BBC).
* Film includes: *Tormented*.
* Private studio includes: Emily Bruni (BBC); Kathryn Drysdale (BBC); Mido Hamada (ABC); William Huston (RSC); Sophie Okonedo (BBC); Toby Stephens (Theatre Royal, Haymarket); Diana Quick (Chichester Festival); Indira Varma (Donmar Warehouse).

HighTide's hands-on approach reminds us that a play is the sum of all the investment in it.
Financial Times.

HighTide exists to source, develop and produce new playwrights, pairing these emerging artists with leading mentors from within the industry. We premiere our productions in Suffolk, offering our writers, directors and actors the rare opportunity to début a full realisation of their work before an audience prior to further development in national tours and transfers.

The first HighTide Festival in 2007 premiered eight short plays written by Tom Basden, Steven Bloomer, Sarah Cuddon, Sam Holcroft, Matthew Morrison, Pericles Snowdon, Megan Walsh and Iain Weatherby.

Tom Basden's *Assembly* then transferred to the Hay-on-Wye Festival 2008.

The second HighTide Festival in 2008 premiered four plays written by Adam Brace, Joel Horwood, Nick Payne and the fourth devised by the company You Need Me.

Joel Horwood's *I Caught Crabs in Walberswick* transferred to Edinburgh Festival Fringe 2008, a UK tour, and the Bush Theatre, in a co-production with Eastern Angles.

You Need Me's *Certain Dark Things* transferred to BAC.

Adam Brace's *Stovepipe* transferred to West 12 in London as a site-sympathetic production in association with the National Theatre and the Bush Theatre.

Nick Payne's *The Pitch* premiered at Latitude Festival 2008, Suffolk.

The third HighTide Festival in 2009 will feature three premieres, including plays by Lucy Caldwell and Jesse Weaver.

Tickets for HighTide Festival 2009 on sale March 1.
www.hightide.org.uk

For HighTide

The 3 rd
HighTide Festival

The Cut / Halesworth / Suffolk / 27 April - 10 May 2009

Three premiere productions including

Plus

Lucy Caldwell's *Guardians*.
Directed by Natalie Abrahami.

Jesse Weaver's *Muhmah*.
Directed by Steven Jon Atkinson.

David Hare's *Berlin and Wall*,
directed by Stephen Daldry;
One Evening - Schubert's *Winterreise*
with text by Samuel Beckett, directed
by Katie Mitchell and produced by
Aldeburgh Music;
British Film Through the Decades -
features Q & A sessions with leading
directors, writers and actors.

Full programme announced
and tickets on sale March 1
www.hightide.org.uk

HighTide is a registered charity and is dependant on the ongoing support of individuals, businesses and charitable trusts & foundations.

HighTide is proud to be supported by:

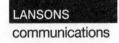
communications

Leading corporate sponsor: Lansons Communications

JERWOOD **SPACE**

Subsidised rehearsal space provided by Jerwood Space

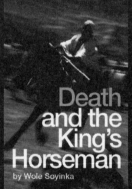

Bush Theatre

'One of the most experienced prospectors of raw talent in Europe'
The Independent

For thirty-nine years, the Bush Theatre has pursued its singular vision of discovery, risk and entertainment from its home in Shepherd's Bush. That vision is valued and embraced by a community of audience and artists radiating out from our distinctive corner of West London across the world. The Bush is a local theatre with an international reputation. Since its inception, the Bush has produced hundreds of groundbreaking premieres, many of them Bush commissions, and hosted guest productions by leading companies and artists from across the world. On any given night, those queuing at the foot of our stairs to take their seats could have travelled from Auckland or popped in from round the corner.

What draws them to the Bush is the promise of a good night out and our proven commitment to launch, from our stage, successive generations of playwrights and artists. Stephen Poliakoff, Victoria Wood, Catherine Johnson, Jonathan Harvey, Tony Kushner, David Eldridge, Samuel Adamson and Jack Thorne (all then unknown) began their careers at the Bush. The unwritten contract between talent and risk is understood by actors who work at the Bush, creating roles in untested new plays. Unique amongst local theatres, the Bush consistently draws actors of the highest reputation and calibre. Joseph Fiennes and Ian Hart recently took leading roles in a first play by an unknown playwright to great critical success. Richard Wilson and John Simm acted in premiers both of which transferred into the West End. The Bush has won over 100 awards, and developed an enviable reputation for touring its acclaimed productions nationally and internationally.

Audiences and organisations far beyond our stage profit from the risks we take. The value attached to the Bush by other theatres and by the film and television industries is both significant and considerable. The Bush receives more than 1,000 scripts through the post every year, and reads and responds to them all. This is one small part of a comprehensive playwrights' development programme which nurtures the relationship between writer and director, as well as playwright residencies and commissions. Everything that we do to develop playwrights focuses them towards a production on our stage or beyond.

We have also launched an ambitious new education, training and professional development programme, bushfutures, providing opportunities for different sectors of the community and professionals to access the expertise of Bush playwrights, directors, designers, technicians and actors, and to play an active role in influencing the future development of the theatre and its programme. Over the next three years we aim to increase the reach and impact of the work we do by seeking out and developing networks for writers using digital technology and the internet. Through this pioneering work, the Bush will reach and connect with new writers and new audiences.

Josie Rourke
Artistic Director

The West 12 Centre is pleased

to sponsor this production of

Stovepipe

and wishes the show every success.

Where quality meets convenience

Dear Lindsay, Pleased you enjoyed the Show. Thanks for coming along

Adam Brace
Stovepipe

ff

faber and faber

First published in 2009
by Faber and Faber Limited
74–77 Great Russell Street
London WC1B 3DA

Typeset by Country Setting, Kingsdown, Kent CT14 8ES
Printed in England by CPI Bookmarque Ltd, Croydon, Surrey

A CIP record for this book
is available from the British Library

ISBN 978-0-571-25057-8

2 4 6 8 10 9 7 5 3 1

This play is dedicated to Diane Brace
with thanks and love

Acknowledgements

The play itself was shaped by the advice and
dramaturgy of Jack Bradley and John Ginman

The play also benefited enormously
from the input of Michael Longhurst and the cast

Seb Armesto has believed in it from the start

Saad Al-Masri, Sebastian Born and Gareth Jandrell
have all been, in different ways, instrumental

I'd also like to thank the employees of the
private security companies that I met in Amman;
my agent Rosie Cobbe; Mark, Sam and Steven at
HighTide; Thom Disney; Suzanne Bell; the gentlemen
of Flat 84 The Woolhouse; Fin Kennedy
and all the writers from Goldsmiths

Finally, I'd specially like to thank three teachers,
to whom I'm indebted:

John Ginman at Goldsmiths
Alan Pearlman at Kent
Brian Joplin at St John's

Agb

Author's Notes

Doubling

The play was originally written as
an ensemble piece for five actors.

ALAN	*male*
SAAD / RAMI / VARIOUS	*Arab male*
EDDY / HARRY / VARIOUS	*white male*
MASHA / SALLY / CAROLYN	*female*
ANDRE / GRIF / VARIOUS	*white male*

Punctuation

'*Full silence*' is a silence in which words
are actively not said.

'*Silence*' is a silence in which there is nothing
to be said.

An oblique stroke (/) indicates
that the next line should begin at this point.

Otherwise, punctuation is to aid delivery –
for example, no question mark indicates
that the sentence is not intoned as a question.

Characters

Alan Dobbs, English

Eddy Wallace, Scottish

Andre Classens, South African

Carolyn Classens, English

Saad Rahim, Iraqi

Chris 'Grif' Griffiths, Welsh

Masha, Russian

Marty, Canadian

Harry, English

Rami, Lebanese-Australian

Sally Steiger, American

Tareq, Egyptian

Arab Businessman, from a Gulf State

Ambrose, British

Walsh, British

Arab Man and numerous **Conference Exhibitors**

STOVEPIPE

A 'stovepipe' is a common firearm malfunction.
It occurs when shooting a firearm with a limp wrist.
This causes the muzzle to rise excessively,
in turn resulting in the case not being ejected.

Act One

ONE: REBUILD IRAQ

The audience are welcomed as delegates to the Project Rebuild Iraq Conference. Harry, an Englishman, addresses the audience.

Harry Welcome to the Security Zone of Project Rebuild Iraq. We are delighted to be part of the annual International Rebuild Iraq Conference in Jordan's buzzing capital Amman. As one of our very first keynote speakers, allow me to introduce: a legend in his own lifetime, the original soldier of fortune, Andre Classens!

Andre, a South African man with a walking stick, addresses the audience.

Andre Thank you. Thank you for having me. We are entering a new phase in the future of Iraq.

We have had the surge, now we have the exodus.

When the troops leave Iraq – sooner than they should and not soon enough for some. When the troops leave Iraq, peaceniks the world over will see it as some sort of victory. Their consciences clear, they will forget. They will forget that the job the troops were doing, it did not just disappear.

Possibly I'm preaching to the choir when I say this.

But it's worth saying again. If you want lasting peace in Iraq, you won't do it without electricity.

You won't do it without a system of government.

You won't do it without *international* investment.

And these things are impossible. Impossible.

Without private security companies.

Remember the name of this conference. Remember the point of –

A siren goes off.
Alan, Andre's bodyguard, springs out of nowhere
and knocks Andre to the ground.

TWO: THE CONTRACT

The siren stops abruptly. Everything is still, except for
Alan, who gets up and, after a while, addresses the
audience.

Alan Because I've done regular army and private military
company, people ask me what the difference is.

And you know, the good things about what I do now
are simple.

Now: I get to choose what weapon I use.

Most of the time, I use the same weapons I always
used.

But – (*Smiles.*) I get the choice.

Alan starts reading a contract.
Andre and Carolyn, an Englishwoman, stand away
from him, in another place.

That's bullshit. But it's what I tell people when they ask.

Andre Acknowledgement. Contractor agrees and
acknowledges the hazardous nature of the services to be
provided.

Alan (*to audience*) Our company's run by a South African
bloke. Andre. A legend in this business.

Carolyn The company cannot be held accountable in the
event of a contractor's injury, dismemberment or emotional
distress caused by terrorists or insurgents.

Alan (*to audience*) His wife's involved too. The talk is,
she's the business brain.

Carolyn Or employees of coalition governments –

Alan is reading the contract. He is approached by Eddy, a Scot, and Grif, a Welshman. They have their own contracts. They start cheerfully mocking him.

– known or unknown domestic and foreign citizens, or other independent contractors to the company.

Grif Could this be Alan from the Paras?

Alan (*to audience*) Eddy and Grif were the ones who got me involved.

Eddy What, this ballbag?

Grif He's let himself go.

Eddy Big time.

Grif He looks like a bum.

Alan Great to see you as well, boys.

Eddy This is what happens to these ex-soldiers. I've seen it in a documentary.

Grif Surely he should be usin his *transferable skills.*

Alan I was just thinking the other day –

Grif The Alan I knew wouldn't still be in bed at four in the afternoon.

Alan I miss Grif and Eddy.

Eddy Shitty state of affairs bein still in bed at four in the afternoon.

Alan But I'd forgotten what a pair of cunts you are.

Eddy What would you prescribe, Grif?

Grif I'd prescribe a cash injection n' a bit of fresh desert air.

Eddy That's very wise of you, I think, Grif.

Carolyn Contractor fully appreciates the dangers and voluntarily assumes the following risks.

Grif You gonna read it all? It's pretty long.

Alan You boys haven't read it then.

Eddy Aye, we have.

> *During this exchange Eddy and Grif sign their contract on each other's back and start getting dressed as Private Security Contractors.*

Carolyn Potential threats include –

Grif We're all on the same contract.

Carolyn – being shot, permanently maimed, and or killed by firearms or munitions, falling aircraft or helicopters –

Eddy It's nuthin you wouldn't expect.

Carolyn – sniper fire, landmines, artillery fire, rocket-propelled grenades, truck- or car-bombs –

Eddy You're voluntarily walkin into the middle of a shitstorm.

Carolyn – poisoning, civil uprising –

Eddy Can't complain if you get shit on your face.

Carolyn – earthquakes or other natural disasters, hearing loss, eye injury or loss, damage to skin, teeth or hair. Terrorist activity, hand-to-hand combat, disease, plane or helicopter crash –

Alan There must be a catch somewhere.

Carolyn – inhalation or contact with airborne or surface biological or chemical contaminants –

Alan starts getting dressed as a Private Security Contractor.

Alan Six hundred dollars a day. Twenty-four hours seven days a week job, turns six hundred dollars a day, into – What? Six hundred by twenty-four, that's –

Eddy Twelve is fifty. Twenty-five.

Alan Twenty-five dollars. Fifteen pound an hour, that is. That's a waiter in a fancy restaurant.

Eddy (*beat*) With tips.

Alan With tips.

Carolyn – or injury by flying debris, shrapnel or improvised hand-propelled missiles.

Eddy You're the one with debts comin out your dick.

Carolyn It is the specific responsibility of the contractor to obtain personal insurance.

Grif You miss it anyway.

Alan What do I miss again?

Eddy The buzz.

Alan Do I really?

Eddy Yeah, but you like to think you dinnae.

Alan I like to think –

Grif Too fuckin much.

Alan I like to think that in some small way, by going out there and doing this work, with the people of Iraq, that I can really. Help. Pay off my dead parents' farming debts.

Alan signs on Eddy's back.

Carolyn Failure to fulfil any of the stipulated duties may lead to legal action.

Eddy Welcome to the firm.

Alan clasps hands with both Grif and Eddy.
Grif and Eddy exit.

THREE: THE AIRPORT RUN

Alan addresses the audience.

Alan My father once told me that the most dangerous road in the world was in Bolivia, twelve thousand feet up a mountain. They call it El Camino de la Muerte. Or Road of Death.

Alan is now the rear gunner in an armoured vehicle on Route Irish. Grif is driving it. Eddy is front gunner.

Every day in Baghdad, we do the airport run. A convoy to pick up anyone who pays, or anything that's paid for.
The airport road's called Route Irish.
Maybe cos the other name was taken.

Music with a bass kicks in.

Grif ALL WEAPONS RED.

Eddy Roger that.

Alan (*to audience*) I rack the fifty-cal, safety off. (*To team.*) Done.

Grif Everyone man their sector.

From here, all communication between the team is over radio. Alan speaks to the team on radio and the audience without.

Grif Okay, let's get the fuck outta dodge.

They move off.

Alan (*to audience*) There's a shit loada charred date trees lining Irish.

Eddy Let's accelerate through this.

Alan (*to audience*) You gotta look in 'em for homemades.

Eddy ALL CLEAR.

Alan (*to audience*) On a feeder road there's a pile of cooked out BMW carcasses.

Eddy ALL CLEAR.

Alan (*to audience*) The ground's all scorched.

Grif J Bridge!

Eddy STILL CLEAR.

Alan (*to audience*) The first bridge, called J for Jihad.

Grif Remember the morning briefing, watch for I.E.D.s under the bridge.

Alan (*to audience*) Eddy scans for I.E.D.s, improvised exploding devices, that could be hidden in the gutters or the shadows.

Eddy CLEAR.

Grif Bastard principal's right up my arse.

Alan (*to audience*) We're escortin a truck carrying building materials.

Eddy Wave him back, Al.

Alan (*to audience, waving*) For new police stations going up in Baghdad.

Grif Traffic fucking everywhere.

Alan (*to audience*) When your principal's a truck, you can't hide what you are.

Eddy *Imshi!* [Get away!]

Alan (*to audience*) So we make a big noise, take a big gun and make a big show of bein happy to use it.

Eddy *IMSHI! IMSHI!*

Alan *IMSHI! IMSHI!*

Eddy *IMSHI!*

Alan (*to audience*) Some know more Arabic than others.

Eddy (*throwing out his fist*) *IMSHI!*

Alan (*to audience*) We all know 'Imshi'.

Eddy *IMSHI! IMSHI!* (*Under his breath.*) Get back, for the love of God.

Grif Give 'em a warning.

Eddy fires off a few warning shots in front of the offending vehicle.

CLEAR THE BRIDGE!

Eddy Roger.

Alan GUNS UP 'N' OUT.

Eddy and Alan aim their guns at the bridge and then back down.

Grif Okay, possible I.E.D.s. Scan for unusuals.

Eddy Oncoming. Four people in a taxi. (*Fist out.*) IMSHI! IMSHI!

Alan (*to audience*) Passing the Saddam Monument, we enter the Kill Zone.

Eddy Okay, we're in the shitbox now, let's burn through it.

Alan (*to audience*) There are charts, in all the pretty colours you want –

Eddy (*determined*) CLEAR!

Alan (*to audience*) – showing more of us die on this stretch than –

Gunshots crack out around their heads, Alan ducks.

Eddy Fuck.

Alan (*shaken*) Where's the sniper? WHERE'S THE SNIPER!

Eddy Nothing in view, sit tight.

Grif Were we engaged just then?

Alan (*team*) Yeah, we're through it. (*To audience, breathless*) Up ahead a car brakes. Another darts towards us –

Grif CHECK HIM OUT!

Eddy Eyes on.

Grif CHECK HIM THE FUCK OUT!

Alan (*to audience*) We look for nervous driver, dressed in white, clean-shaven.

Eddy *IMSHI! IMSHI!* Okay, he's fallin back.

Grif Keep 'im goin.

Eddy CLEAR!

Grif Okay, we're looking good now.

Eddy Let's not count our cunts afore they're fucked.

Grif Hold tight, almost home.

Alan (*to audience*) Route Irish is a lot safer than it was.

Eddy Let's make it nice and clean from here.

Grif Last scan for I.E.D.s, gents.

Alan (*to audience*) The Yanks have given it a workin over and it's not / as dangerous –

Eddy FUCK I SEEN ONE ELEVEN O'CLOCK *DON'T* –

Grif WHAT / THE FUCK!

Eddy I.E.D.

Alan FUCK!!

Grif FUCK!!

> *They all brace themselves as they run over something that could've been an I.E.D.*
> *They register they're alive. They're in shock.*
> *Silence.*

Alan Was that a fuckin Big Mac wrapper?

> *Silence.*

Grif I think it was a Whopper.

Eddy Was that. Some prize cunt's dropped a Whopper box in the middle / of the road!

Grif Jesus Christ, why didn't we see that earlier.

Alan I don't think Whoppers come in boxes.

Eddy Let's decide what the fuck it was later –

Grif I think they do, they – CLEAR?

Eddy ALL CLEAR.

Grif I think they come in, no! No / they come in that –

Alan Whoppers come in that silvery –

Grif – silvery, yeah, / paper.

Eddy Keep your HEADS ON. I don't wanna be talking about fuckin hamburgers.

Alan Whoa whoa, he's slowin up.

Grif (*in rear-view mirror*) What the fuck's he doin?

  Alan is frantically waving at the truck to keep moving.
  Car horns can be heard, one of them Grif's.

Alan (*to audience*) The convoy should be goin flat out,
but the Iraqi lad drivin the truck's slowin to a standstill.
(*Gesturing.*) Keep movin, y' bastard!

Eddy What sort of a total gangfuck does this look like?

Grif Think it's a come-on?

Alan (*to audience*) First thought is it's a trap, and the
local militia are in on it.

Grif You told 'im, don't fuckin stop whatever 'appens.

Eddy You heard me.

Alan (*to audience*) If this was a British military operation,
we'd have radio contact with the truck. And we'd know
its driver. But it isn't, and we don't.

Grif Well then, he's on the mudjahadeen payroll and
we're leavin 'im.

  Grif goes to drive off.

Alan No, no, he's waving at us. He's pointing at the dash.

Grif I don't trust it.

Alan What's the S.O.P. here?

Eddy The S.O.P. is call the cunt up on the comms n' ask
him why he's tryna get us all murdered.

Grif Right, we're leavin him. (*Goes to drive off.*)

Eddy But we don't have any comms, so I'll go n' ask him
myself, how's that?

Grif We're fuckin leavin 'im, Eddy!

Eddy has ducked out of the vehicle.

Grif Fuckin hell, Eddy. This is bullshit!

Alan (*to audience*) We watch Eddy run low, back arched with his hands hangin down. He reaches the cab and I'm almost expectin him to lay the guy out and ask questions later, but he gets in, looks at the dash.

Alan moves out of the car. We can't see the vehicle or Grif or Eddy any more.

He's telling us there's no petrol in the truck. It's insane. They're runnin on empty. It'd even be hilarious, if we weren't sittin on the most dangerous road in the world like it was the hard shoulder of the M4 cos somebody needed a piss.

And I get out there with our spare petrol, and we're pouring it in but we don't have a funnel and it's sprayin everywhere cos we're shaking so hard. And I look up n' Ed's just standin staring back at our vehicle. Then sound, like distortion on a speaker. And the heat of an oven hits us. And I see it. Our vehicle. It's not so much *on* fire.

It is fire.

It's just fire.

That's all it is.

FOUR: SA-DUCK-OO

Alan is sitting in his hotel room at the Intercontinental, Amman.

Alan (*to audience*) When a diver's goin to the depths, he has to go slowly. On the way down he stops for a minute or two, treads water. Lets his body get used to the conditions.

That's what Amman is for contractors.
After Iraq. And before. We tread water.

Eddy stuns him with a stun gun. Alan drops to the floor screaming in pain. Marty, a Canadian man, enters.

Marty What the fuck is going on?

Alan is groaning and laughing.

Eddy The stun guns work.

Marty You just stunned this guy?

Eddy Aye.

They both look at Alan recovering on the floor.

Marty I can't believe you just stunned this guy. You know this guy's gotta be fresh tomorrow. You alright?

Alan Not really.

Eddy He's makin a meal of it.

*Alan moves suddenly and stuns Eddy in the leg.
    Eddy yelps and drops to the floor, laughing and writhing in pain.*

Marty Stop stunning each other with these goddamn stun guns!

They continue as if he hadn't said anything.

Eddy *Fuck*, that hurts! I didn't do you in the leg at least.

They are both lying on the floor now, laughing and recovering. Marty is incredulous.

Just testin our equipment out, Marty. Gotta be careful with this company, never know what's gonna be made of shite.

Marty I never had any problem with any company kit.

Alan gestures to Marty not to continue.

Look, just. Keep it down. Crazy as it sounds, some guys like sleep before they drive into a war zone.

Marty leaves. Alan crawls to get a beer, opens it and hands it to Eddy. They share it.

Eddy If you had to go. Out here. What's your best way?

Alan Tough.

Eddy But?

Alan Go down fighting. Save the principal. Who is a beautiful journalist. From America. She writes a book about me.

Eddy Sickening.

Alan You?

Eddy Fist fight wi' Osama Bin Laden. On a volcano.
I punch him into the moutha the volcano.
But the force of ma punch carries me with him.
The volcano erupts.

Alan (*beat, amused*) Not a lotta volcanoes in Iraq, Eddy.

Eddy Not a lotta Osama Bin Laden either, Alan. As we now know.

Eddy holds the bottle up in a toast.

Grif.

He drinks and hands it to Alan, who drinks.

Alan Grif.

*Alan hands the beer back to Eddy and gets up to pack.
There's a sudoku puzzle on the table. Alan sees it and throws a look at Eddy. Eddy's not watching so Alan carefully turns it over.*

Eddy I been meanin to say.

Alan Uh-huh.

Eddy The Aussie in the other team thinks you're gonna flake. Says you got flake written on your foreheed.

Alan What, like a Cadbury's advert.

Eddy No, like a guy who's gonna walk out on a deployment.

Alan Well, I'm not.

Full silence.

Eddy This ain't a big fuckin heart-to-heart or nothing but, after Grif n that. It would be kinda justified.

Alan I've come back out here, haven't I?

Eddy If you did flake, it would fuck us. Wouldn't it?

Alan I expect it would, yeah.

Eddy For about a week. Tops. Then they'd just forget about you.
   Ah, I'm just drunk.

Full silence.

That driver coulda known the guy who siphoned his tank.

Alan (*sigh*) So say he did, say it was a plan. They siphoned his petrol and he knew about it. How'd he know where he was gonna stop? And when. He'd run completely dry, he wasn't fuckin us about. It was bad luck. Someone got him at the airport when he wasn't looking and suddenly, no petrol.
   And if he was springin an ambush, d'you think he'd have more in the way of backup than one twelve-year-old, fuckin –

Eddy Alright.
   All I'll say is, with radio contact, wouldna happened.

Alan (*beat*) Possibly.

Eddy You've gotta have comms in that situation.

Alan The driver didn't speak any English, Ed. (*Beat.*) D'we have to rake over it again.

Full silence. Eddy sees the paper on the table.

Eddy What's this you're up to, eh?

Alan Nothin much. Readin the paper.

Eddy What paper?

Alan *Jordan Times.*

Eddy turns it over and finds the sudoku.

Eddy Sa-duck-oo!

Alan (*sheepish*) Yeah.

Eddy You're doin a fuckin sa-duck-oo?

Alan Yeah.

Eddy We went out on the lash and you stayed in doin a fuckin sa-duck-oo?

Alan Yes.

Eddy shakes his head, disgusted.

Eddy Well, you mighta photocopied it for me.

Alan (*beat*) Come on.

Eddy You know how much I like a fuckin sa-duck-oo.

Alan Where was I gonna photocopy it in Amman at this hour?

Eddy You're in a *hotel*, you think hotels don't have fuckin *photocopiers*? Conference comin to town, suits everywhere you look, and you couldnae lay you hands on a *photocopier*?

28

Alan You can finish it if you're so –

Eddy grabs the paper.

Eddy You probably fucked it already. What can I do if you've fucked it up already? Every decision I make's based on a false. Fuckin.

Alan Pretext.

Eddy Pretext, aye.

Alan Not if you start from the beginning / and check.

Eddy You scribbled all over it! I've got half a booka these to last me six weeks.

Alan I think you might be overreacting.

Eddy That's less than one a day.

He staggers around angrily for a few moments.

Alan Maybe you could download some.

Masha, a Russian, walks into Alan's room.

You can download them, can't you?

They see her.

Masha Excuse me.

She points to her watch and talks to Eddy.

The time. Thirty minutes, gone.

Eddy (*completely unembarrassed*) Yeah, fine.

Masha I sit down, wait, thirty minutes.

Eddy Yeah, I've been havin a chat with my pal.

Alan Hello.

Eddy This is my Russian friend.

Alan shakes her hand cordially.

Alan Very nice to meet you.

Masha (*cold*) Please to meet you. (*To Eddy.*) When you come back, time not start. Now, only thirty minutes, yes?

Eddy I've said fine.

Alan That'll be more than enough, honestly.

Masha (*shrugs*) Okay, I wait.

She leaves.

Alan She's what you meant when you said you were getting takeaway.

Eddy I always say takeaway.

Alan But you say takeaway for both prostitutes *and* food.

Eddy But if I say Russian takeaway, you can make an educated fuckin guess that I'm not talking about beetroot soup.
Alright.

Eddy is about to leave and turns back and hugs Alan.

You're a good pal.

They cling to each other.

But you shoulda let me do the sa-duck-oo.

Eddy throws Alan onto the floor.
They wrestle.
Alan ends it by flipping Eddy over and lying on him, putting him in a lock.

Alan I'm tired, mate, if I let you up, are you gonna do that again?

Eddy Let me up.

Alan does and Eddy gets up and walks out, upset.

Alan See you at breakfast.

Alan watches him go.

FIVE: LAST BREAKFAST

Breakfast is being served at the Intercontinental. Marty is eating an enormous bowl of cereal.

Alan (*to audience*) On the morning you go in, you don't like to talk much. Especially, you don't wanna talk about the job.

Marty spots him.

(*To audience.*) Most guys understand this.

Marty Hey Al! Al ma pal!

Marty waves at him to come and sit down.

Alan Hey Marty. Eddy been down yet?

Marty Han't seen him. Hey, we gotta get our asses oota this job soon huh.

Marty laughs through his cereal. Alan starts making a call.

I'm stayin in the saddle till I get this custody case going, I told you I'm tryna get in a custody case for my daughter? That's why I missed that rotation, the rotation when you guys lost – What was his name?

Alan Grif. (*Into phone.*) As I leave this, you are missin the last chance to eat western food for about three hundred miles. (*Hangs up.*)

Marty Grif. Yeah. Man that was fucked, I was so sorry to hear boot that. I know people say it's safer, but we're still losing guys.

Marty gets his phone out and brings up an image.

That's. That's my daughter there.

Alan Very nice. How old's she?

Marty No no, it's a video, play it.

Alan Okay.

He does so, and squints to make out the picture.

Marty She's six.

Alan What's that she's. Is she hitting an animal?

Marty She's just playing.

Alan But she's hit the dog square in the face.

Marty No, the dogs love her, it's a game. It's a game they play.

Alan I had a dog and I played with her every day and not once did I hit her square in the face.

Marty Well. Every dog's different, Jesus Christ!

Alan nods and hands the phone back.

So here's me makin one-eighty a year Canadian, my wife's makin one-twenny. And she ain't getting shot at.
 Irony is, she'll use my job against me in court. Mercenary father versus caring mother. You better believe it.
 I mean, in five centuries, y'know, they're not gonna care about my wife's fuckin gourmet sandwich company. But Iraq. Iraq will matter. Like Andre says.

Alan Unless those sandwiches are pretty fuckin special.

Marty No man. She doesn't fill them up to the crusts.

Alan makes another call.

Alan (*into phone*) Hello, mate. You're missing breakfast. (*He listens, frowning. Into phone.*) Mm-hmm.

Marty Tell him to getta move on.

Alan (*into phone*) Where are you?

Alan gets up, moves away from Marty.

SIX: MASHA

The streets of downtown Amman. Masha is waiting.
Alan walks over to her, a steely urgency in his manner.

Alan Alright, where is he?

Masha (*yawns*) Phone is here.

Alan Eddy is not in the hotel.

Masha I tell you this.

Alan So where the fuck is he?

Masha He not say to me.

Alan Was he kidnapped?

Masha No.

Alan He just walked out.

Masha He walk out, actually he leave before I leave. I have the shower and he walk out.

Alan Tell me what happened before that.

Masha He was sad, and he was drunken, and we have sex, and then he pack bag and he go. And he give me phone.

33

Full silence. Alan looks at her.

I am very tired – I can get money now?

Alan He's meant to be leaving Amman with me in twenty minutes.

Masha You want phone?

Alan He *packed his bag*?

Masha Yes, you want phone?

Alan Yeah, give me the phone. (*Getting money out.*) What did he say to you?

Masha He say many things.

Alan What?

Masha He say he like me to, sit on his face. And he say I am beautiful / and dirty.

Alan What did he say about him leaving?

Masha Nothing.

They exchange phone and money.

Alan Look me in the eyes. He walked out?

Masha playfully pulls her eyes wide and moves her face to his.

Masha Ye–es. Why I lie? Where you think he go to?

Alan He can't go anywhere. He hasn't got his passport.

Masha Why not?

Alan The company has it. It's the way things are done.

He sighs. Looks at his watch.

Did you ask him where he was going?

Masha He leave when I am shower.

Alan So you didn't see him go?

Masha No.

Alan So someone could've come and taken him?

Masha (*shrugs*) Maybe I would hear this.

Alan Were there any, any local men, any Arab men in the corridor?

Masha No no. I tell you I see him pack bag.

Alan You work for the Russian bar, right?

Masha I work for myself, and bar.
  I'm sorry your friend run away. He was okay, nice man.

Alan Yeah, I know.

He looks at Masha and takes her arm suddenly.

Alan Are you – Is this a mafia thing?

Masha (*scoffs*) Okay, nice to meet you.

She goes to leave and turns back angrily.

From Russia so *of course* I must be mafia bitch.
  Well.

> *She flips him the middle finger.*
> *Alan tries to say something, but Masha strides out, disdainfully.*
> *Alan starts to look at Eddie's phone. Gets out his own phone and makes a call.*

Alan (*into his phone*) Marty. Eddy's not gonna be at the meet. (*Beat.*) I'm not gonna be there either. Go on without us and we'll see you in Baghdad. (*Beat*) Don't ask, that's just how it is.

Jordanian pop music begins loudly.

SEVEN: UNDERCOVER SCHOOL

A bar in an expensive hotel in Amman. The pop music is now in the background. There is an Arab barman, Tareq. Sally, an American, sits in the bar. She has a notebook or a laptop. Two PSCs, Walsh and Ambrose, enter chatting.

Walsh Taxi man tried to scam us again.

Ambrose Twenty JD for a trip downtown.

One of Ambrose or Walsh starts singing, the other picking it up quickly. They are singing for themselves, but with an eye on Sally and the ladies in the bar.

Both (*to the tune of 'Downtown' by Tony Hatch*)
When you're alone and life is making you lonely
You can always go:
BANGDAD!
Think you got worries, those Shias n the Sunnis
Have it worse I know!
BANGDAD!
Listen to the firefights by the filthy River Tigris!
Dust and sand are in your eyes, it is a desert climate!

Ambrose (*solo*) How can you sleep?

Both
The air is much thinner there
'N' you can't work your air con
But do not despair,
You're in
BANGDAD!
Contractors' graveyard called
BANGDAD!

Alan has entered during the song. He's drunk and imbued with a sardonic confidence. He unashamedly looks at Sally.

Your family'd be appalled
BANGDAD!

Ambrose
Al-Quaeda are waiting for
Yoooouuuuu.

Both
Bangdad. Bangdad.

Ambrose does the horn end bit.

Bangdad. Bangdad.

They laugh. Alan is still looking at Sally and she's noticed.

Sally Hi. Have we met?

Alan We have now.

Sally I guess so.

Alan Yeah.

Sally Well, how about that – it was great to meet you.

She turns away from him.

Walsh (*to Ambrose*) I'm gonna go and break the seal. Get another in.

Walsh leaves. Ambrose remains at the bar. Alan stays looking at Sally. He has seen she's wearing a ring.

Alan Cheap wedding ring. To ward off the Arab men.

She's ignoring him.

You heard some horror stories. So. It's your first time in the Middle East. In your bag you've got a headscarf, which you wear when you're not in the hotel. Because you thought you needed to. Stop me when I'm wrong.

Sally (*politely*) I'm gonna stop when you're being offensive which is, uh, actually right now.

Alan And you have a notebook. And you're a bit bolshie. Which means you're a journalist. You don't wear much make-up and you dress a bit like a boy. You're a print journalist. You're American so you could be going anywhere, but you're marginally too pretty to get embedded. So no, so you're gonna go and sit in an air-conditioned room in the Green Zone while the locals do all your work for you. Fuck, I might've even been escorting you if I wasn't here.

Sally nods, taking in this unprovoked attack.

Sally And why are you here?

Alan Secret mission.

Sally Is that so?

Alan Yeah.

Sally Yeah?

Alan I could tell you, but I'd have to fuck you.

Sally (*beat*) Is your secret mission being a real asshole? (*Beat.*) If it is, that's going extremely well.

She looks at him and relaxes. He might be a story.

C'mon, what d'you do? How come you're out here?

Alan (*thinks about saying something, then smiles at her*) At least make an effort. Don't they do undercover school or something.

Sally I'm not undercover.

He looks directly into her eyes.

Alan Would you like to be?

Sally It's *not* a cheap wedding ring.

Alan All wedding rings are cheap out here.

Sally (*beat*) What about your mission?

Alan I've done as much looking as I can.

Sally What are you looking for?

Alan There's someone I'm tryna track down.

Sally In here?

Alan He might come in here.

Sally That's not exactly tracking him down. Waiting for him to maybe show up.

Alan (*defensive*) He likes coming here. This is the best place I can be. This is the number one place.

Full silence.

Sally You're a merc, aren't you.

Alan Nope.

Sally You look like a merc.

Alan And what's a 'merc'?

Sally A 'mercenary'.

Alan And what do they do?

Sally You should know.

Alan I think mercenaries are paid to fight, aren't they? Which doesn't make me a mercenary, because I'm paid to avoid fights. But then journalists are paid to tell the truth, aren't they? Which is funny cos they sit in little editing suites in well-protected compounds and wouldn't know the truth if it came and put a cock in their pretty mouth.

Sally Wow, aren't we just the root of all evil. (*Beat.*) And FYI, I'm based here. With Reuters. I'm on kidnappings. So, thankfully nothing to do with your crazy little world.

Alan Kidnappings. (*Beat.*) Do you have a number here?

Sally (*laughs*) That's cute, but whad'you take me for exactly?

Alan No really, I might know someone. I might, uh. I'm looking for a mate of mine, Ed Wallace.

Sally Okay, that's highly comic, but I'm not going to bed with you.

Alan For real. He disappeared off the radar yesterday morning. I thought he'd show up but he hasn't. I've been all over Amman, no sign.

She looks at him with a kind of pity. Walsh enters singing and Ambrose joins in.

Walsh
Que sera sera,

Both
Whatever will be will be.
We're goina Bas*ra* City,
Que s'Iraq! S'Iraq!

Sally If he's really been kidnapped, I'll find you, how about that.

Tareq Gentlemen, please. The customers, they don't want to hear you sing, I think.

Sally Now. Oughtn't you to go back to your *boys*?

Alan Hmm?

Sally Aren't you with them?

Alan looks around, sees the singing men.

Alan (*quietly*) No.

Ambrose Tell your manager we're not singing any more.

Walsh (*sings*) Any more!

Both (*to the tune of 'Bread of Heaven'*)
We're not singing any more, any – more!

Tareq has left to get his manager.

We're not singing any more.

Ambrose (*to Alan*) Oi, sing up, Lone Ranger.

Both
We're not singing any more, any-more!
We're not singing any more.

They laugh. Sally has left. Jordanian rock music begins loudly.

EIGHT: INTRODUCTIONS

Alan is in an office/business suite in Amman. The Jordanian rock music is now coming from a further room. Saad, an Iraqi, enters.

Saad You wait for Carolyn?

Alan Yeah.

Saad She come soon I think.

Alan Great.

Silence.

Saad You are British, yes?

Alan Yeah.

Saad Before, I am interpreter with British Army.

Alan Oh no way, which regiment?

Saad Royal Dragoons.

Alan Well shit. They're a good solid regiment. Good history.

Alan moves to shake his hand.

I'm Alan. Parachute Regiment. Was.

Saad shakes his hand. Carolyn strides in, on the phone.

Saad Saad. Nice to meet you.

*Another man in a tie carries some documents on,
hands a document in Arabic to Saad and departs. Saad
studies the document.*

Carolyn (*to Alan, hand over handset*) I don't even know
why you're here. I'm too busy to be dealing with fuck-
ups. (*Into phone.*) Okay, which side of Canada? When
can he get here by? Sorry, bear with me. (*Hand over
phone, calling.*) Shut that shit off! Saad, can you go and
tell them to shut that shit off.

Saad sighs and exits.

(*Into phone.*) Well, that's too late. He'd be horrendously
jetlagged. He'd be no good to us. (*Beat.*) Who else?
Okay, well someone without conference experience then.
(*Beat.*) Call me back.

*The music's been turned off. She hangs up and looks at
Alan.*

Alan Have there been any ransom demands?

Carolyn No. And I don't believe there will be. I believe
Wallace walked out and you've exacerbated it by being
criminally stupid. And in order to paper over the cracks
in what is already a contract on the very edge of being
unworkable, I had to send Paul Berg to Baghdad.

Saad wanders back in, nonchalantly.

Alan (*beat*) Do I know him?

Carolyn I don't think you want to. He's intent on breaking
at least one of your legs. (*Beat.*) Paul is Andre's personal
bodyguard and one of our senior conference delegates.

Alan Andre needs a bodyguard? The bloke goes into the jungle to wage a one-man war, but you can't let him walk round a conference hall.

Carolyn Andre is at home in a jungle, he is not at home in a conference hall. Why did Wallace walk out?

Alan I don't know.

Carolyn What about the steroids?

Alan I knew he took a few things.

Carolyn A few? Saad, can you find me, it's in the top right drawer of my other desk, it's a medical record. Family name, Wallace – first name?

Alan Edward.

Saad I am not secretary.

Carolyn (*beat*) No, but you're here to help me, aren't you.

Saad I am here only for translation.

Carolyn But, right now, you're not doing anything.

Saad I am reading.

Carolyn But you're not helping me communicate with anyone, are you?

Saad Of course, nobody is speaking Arabic.

Carolyn looks at Saad intent on a riposte, but gives up.

Carolyn (*to Alan*) Well, in his last medical there's something about a warning to cut down on his steroid intake.

Alan I don't think it was roid rage.

Carolyn What was it then?

Alan We watched a bloke we knew burn to death in his vehicle. And we couldn't get the body out, cos we would've got picked off.

Our principal had his petrol siphoned out of his tank at the airport. He couldn't tell us cos we didn't have comms with him. While we were goin static, boy of about twelve took a lucky shot with a Molotov.

Full silence. Saad is been paying close attention.

Carolyn I know about Chris Griffiths. You think that was it?

Alan No.

Carolyn No?

Alan No. If anything, that made him want to stay even more. Look, can I get back into Baghdad to join up with my team?

Carolyn No, they don't trust you, why should they. I don't trust you. I don't even think you trust yourself. Why don't you say to me 'I can't take it any more'? Then I might have sympathy.

Alan (*beat*) Could I talk to Andre?

Carolyn It's my decision, and Andre's in London seeing a knee specialist.

Alan (*quietly*) Paul Berg get to him, did he.

Carolyn He has ligament damage.

Alan Thought he wasn't active any more.

Carolyn He doesn't deploy any more, no. It's from squash. Or do I mean badminton. I mean badminton.

Her phone rings.

The one with the feather thing.

Alan (*beat*) Yeah, that's badminton.

Saad That is badminton.

Carolyn (*she takes the call*) Mm-hm. (*Sighs.*) Can't you get me anyone? (*Beat.*) I'm staring at the problem right now. Yes, one of them has turned up, claiming noble motives. (*Beat.*) That's what I said.

She looks at Alan intently, while she listens.

It hadn't occurred to me, no. But that doesn't make it a bad idea.

She approaches Alan and takes him by the cheek.

He possibly is quite articulate. (*To Alan.*) Are you quite articulate?

Alan S'pose.

Carolyn (*into phone*) Yeah. And he's presentable. Ex-British Army, senior NCO. You'd think it wouldn't be beyond him. Give me a couple of minutes. (*Hangs up.*)

Carolyn speaks in staccato, almost-bored quickfire.

Alright. Why am I in Amman?

Alan For the Rebuild Iraq Conference.

Carolyn When is that?

Alan It's. Day after tomorrow, isn't it?

Carolyn Yes. Why's it important we do the job we do?

Alan Because. Because not much would get done otherwise. Why?

Carolyn How come we don't come under Iraqi law?

Alan I thought we did now.

Carolyn Good. How's that changed the way we do our job?

45

Alan Personally, it hasn't.

Carolyn (*beat*) Nice answer. Of course it's changed everything, but. Nice answer. (*Beat.*) Is private security anything new?

Alan (*beat*) I don't understand.

Carolyn As an industry, are we doing anything new?

Alan You tell me, Carolyn.

Carolyn We're nothing new at all. We're the natural extension of outsourcing in the security sector. People outsource their IT, their recruitment, their catering. Corporations, governments outsource their security. We provide a service that prevents American stroke British soldiers flying home in big planes with flags on their coffins. We also keep what little that functions in the country, functioning. So the line is, basically, deal with it. Do you have any smart clothing? Shirts, ties, et cetera?

Alan Nope.

Carolyn Saad? Can you take this man shopping, smart clothes, ties, chinos, good price, yes?

Saad *Shopping?*

Carolyn Yes.

Saad You want me now for shopping?

Carolyn Yes, get good bargain.

Saad raises his hands in resignation.

(*To Alan.*) You need to understand this. I don't want to employ you. However, you just about look the part. We have a lot to cover in two days. First, don't tell Andre why you're in Amman, as far he's concerned: you're Paul's replacement. If you don't want him getting very angry with you, and me, about professional pride. Second.

46

Alan Do I have any choice in this?

Carolyn No, unless you want to walk out now, pay your own way back to London and we'll begin proceedings against you. Do you want to do that?

Alan I want to find Eddy.

Carolyn Second. You look for your friend on your own time, if you really think he isn't in Bangkok getting his balls massaged. You give me total focus until the conference is over, and your major fuck-up may become a minor one.

She looks at him.

Chris Griffiths was a good friend?

Alan I was in the Paras with him. Me, Eddy, him.

Carolyn I hope you felt the arrangements we made were appropriate.

Alan (*beat*) Actually. Yeah.

Carolyn I'm sorry Andre couldn't attend the funeral.

Alan Memorial service. Nothing to bury. (*Beat.*) No, I thought the company was very understanding. In the circumstances. I know his family appreciated it.

Carolyn I'm glad.
  Look, we'll talk more. You'll be sticking close to Andre, making nice with potential and existing clients. Plant us in our niche – elite British firm, high standards, culturally sensitive. (*Beat.*) And if you fuck me around, I will sue the skin off you. Wait here while I get your clearance. Saad will keep you entertained, won't you, Saad?

Saad looks over and smiles insincerely at her.
  Carolyn strides out confidently.

Saad and Alan are left alone. They nod at each other. Silence.

Saad The Americans. Uh. Have a phrase. Ball-breaker.

Alan (*smiles*) She's right, you are gonna keep me entertained.

   Silence.

Saad I am sorry for your friend.

Alan Which one?

Saad The dead one. And the lost one.

Alan Thank you. (*Beat.*) You live here in Amman now, right?

Saad Yes, right.

Alan Could you help me? Find my friend. Ask questions, in Arabic. I've got money.

Saad No. Not now. After the conference, I think, yes.

Alan Excellent. Thank you. (*Beat.*) You must be a good translator with this lot.

Saad (*smiles and nods, beat*) No.

Alan But they pay you well, yes?

Saad Yes, very well.

Alan But you are bad translator?

Saad Yes, very bad.

Alan Okay.

Saad I am not translator, see, I am interpreter.

Alan Yeah, gotcha, so you're a bad translator, but a good interpreter.

Saad No, I am a bad interpreter also.

Alan laughs.

Alan How'd you get the job?

Saad Because Andre, he is a kind man.

Alan Is he?

Saad Because I have to leave Iraq.

Alan He gave you the job because you left Iraq.

Saad Now I work only in Amman. I not go back to Iraq.

Alan You stopped working for us? I mean, the Brits?

Saad One day I get, uh. Email. And the email show me to a website. And I see a movie, of my cousin, at his house, and he open the door. And they pull him out to the street. And in the street. They take a great knife. And open his neck. I see that the movie is two minute more long. I stop the movie.
And I leave Basra, same day. For Amman.

Alan I see.

Saad He was interpreter also. British Army.

Alan silently, solemnly nods. Full silence.

He love British comedy.

Alan again nods.

Mister Bean. You know *Mister Bean*?

Alan (*solemnly*) I know *Mister Bean*.

Saad *Mister Bean* his favourite. You watch?

Alan I've seen some.

Saad One time Mister Bean, he is in the church, he clean his nose on his *pocket*. He pull his pocket and he – (*Mimes wiping his nose.*) Clean it. Then, maybe after one minute, he put a candy in there!

Alan is still solemn, but confused.

The same pocket with the dirt from his nose!

Alan I don't really watch them that much.

Saad If you clean nose in mosque: big trouble!

Silence.

Alan I am sorry about your cousin. We value our interpreters very much.

Saad Many Iraqi men, we love *Mister Bean* and so we want to help British Army.

Alan Is that true?

Saad No. (*Beat.*) It is a joke, for you. I am sorry. It is not true.

Alan About your cousin?

Saad No, about *Mister Bean*. He is not funny.

Alan (*beat*) So your cousin isn't dead?

Saad Oh he is dead. But he did not like *Mister Bean*. If he like *Mister Bean*, I would kill him myself.

Full silence.

Alan I'm sorry I.

Saad *Mister Bean* very simple comedy. (*He grins broadly.*) Many people in Iraq die, not because of Sunni–Shia, because of argument about TV.

It dawns on Alan that Saad is screwing with him.

Alan Well, y'know that's why we invaded? We saw your TV and thought, this is shit, we're gonna invade and make you watch our TV.

Saad And now we have American wrestling. *Smackdown*. This is Freedom.

Alan You should be grateful.

Saad Everybody is grateful.

Alan You should be on you knees thanking me.

Saad Yes, I know, but I am like Andre, I have bad knee.

Alan Badminton?

Saad For me, uh, ping-pong.

They laugh.

(*Smiles.*) British soldiers always like to joke.

Alan Your cousin did die though?

Saad nods and thinks.

Saad I don't know why I joke. About that. No, I think I know.

Alan (*beat*) You must miss home.

Saad Some things.

Alan What do you miss?

Saad The sex. (*Matter of fact.*) In war, there is much sex.

Alan Joke?

Saad No. It's true.

Silence.

Alan I've spent about two years there, I must say I never knew.

Saad (*smiles*) Of course not. One day, we will go back to Iraq. We will all go back when we have a new country.

Alan Do you believe that?

Saad looks straight at Alan. Full silence.
Saad smiles and claps Alan on the back.

Saad You and me, talking about my country – it will not help. One day, it will be safe.

Alan Yeah, well. *Inshallah.* [God willing.]

Saad You know some Arabic?

Alan *Shway bes. Ga'id at'allam.* [Very little. I try to learn.]

Saad Your Arabic very good!

Alan It's not really.

Saad (*beat*) No, of course not really. I flatter you.

Alan laughs.

Where did you learn your bad Arabic?

There is a transition to another time and place.
Alan swiftly grabs an Arab man by the neck and puts a gun in his cheek.

Alan *INZIL!* [Get down!] *Inzil, inzil 'al-ardh!* [Get down, get down on the floor!]

Arab *Ma sawwait shei!* [I've done nothing wrong!]

The lights, sound and scenery have changed to mark the transition.
Alan pushes the man down onto his knees. He resists.

Alan *Ithan la t-gawim. Ma ereed e'awrak.* [So don't resist. I don't want to hurt you.] *INZIL!* [Get down!] *La t-goom illa lemma egillak.* [I'll tell you when to get up.]

The man's resistance ceases. Alan puts his gun away and stops. He looks up at the audience, pleased with himself. The Arab man gets up. He is a Lebanese Australian called Rami. It was a role-play presentation in a training camp.

Rami Okay, not bad, uh?

Alan Alan.

Rami Alan, mostly: that was good. (*To audience.*) So you see, good positioning, maybe don't go for the cheek, but physically – that was strong. To dominate the contact you need to use your Arabic, they won't expect you to know any. So Alan's accent – not great, but the Arabic itself – I liked. They teach you that in Basra did they, fella?

Alan Yeah. Y'know. Hearts n' minds.

Rami (*smiles*) Right.
(*To audience.*) So. Do, seriously, work on the fuckin accent because it can and *will* save you a shitloada grief.

Alan joins Grif and Eddy in the audience. Rami goes to a flip chart.

Okay, listen up, this session is the *last* time you will go through *any* of this stuff, before you're deployed. It *is* a short training period, but as a company we trust you to deal with that.

So. Let's whip through this one more time. Private Security Detail. Basics. The CAT vehicle has a load plan for: crew-served weapons, extra ammo, jack, medical kit, litter. What else?

Rami turns to the flip chart.

Grif Grenades?

Rami writes 'Grenades'.

53

Rami Yep.

Eddy Night vision. Other optics.

Rami Good.

Rami writes 'Optics'.

Alan Smoke.

Rami writes 'Smoke bombs'.

Grif (*faux American*) Gas.

Rami starts to write 'G—'. He stops. The boys snigger.

Rami Gas masks?

Grif No, just gas.

Rami Okay. Like. Like gas equipment, chem equipment?

Grif No, gas, for the vehicle. So it'll run.

Rami Gas. Like Gasoline?
    Okay so. So gas. Yeah that's – (*Sighs.*) That's already in there. What else?

Eddy Communication equipment.

Rami writes 'Comms'.

Rami Sure. With your team.

Eddy We'll be commed up with the principal too, right?

Rami Y'know, not often. Fellas, you're gonna be in difficult situations without technology you're used to. Wakey wakey, it's a tough gig. (*Beat.*) What else?

Eddy Chewing gum.

Rami *Chewing* gum?

Eddy For nervous energy. Helps to divert nervous energy.

Rami Okay, let's – Let's just say that the CAT vehicle already has fuckin chewing gum and mint imperials and whatever other little. *Touches* you can think of. And let's say it has a full tank of petrol, and an axle, and fuckin wheels. Okay? Or is that beyond everyone's imagination.

What else? What else d'you want in there?

Alan A bird.

Eddy Drinks cabinet.

Grif Sky Sports.

Rami Yeah, laugh it up, fellas. I hope you're still havin this much fun months from now, I really do.

There is a transition to another time and place. The lights go a lot darker.

Alan, Eddy and Grif are shining torches and yelling at the audience, who are a crowd.

Eddy *Imshi! Imshi!* [Get away!]

Alan Fuck me, where did this lot spring from.

Eddy, Alan and Grif hold this conversation in snatches while they are shouting Arabic at the crowd. They use phrases like:

The Boys *Irja'.* [Get back.]
Imshi hnaak. [Go over there.]
Irja' baitek. [Please go home.]

Alan Are they protesting?

Grif They're breakin the curfew, whetever they're doin. What's Arabic for curfew?

Eddy Al, what's Arabic for curfew?

Alan Do I look like a walkin fuckin Arabic dictionary?

Grif Pay attention of these fuckers.

Grif starts being overzealous in his treatment of the crowd.

Alan (*to Eddy*) Have a word, will you.

Eddy Grif, stay calm, pal.

More shouts in Arabic until the crowd is dispersed.
A moment of calm.
They're on their own.

Alan Don't they want the police station finished?

Eddy Fuck knows what they want.

Grif (*to Eddy*) Don't tell me to stay calm when we're dealing with a mass of natives in the pitch black.

Eddy Aye, well.

Eddy and Grif have a moment of quiet stand-off.
As a result, they don't notice a figure breaking from the darkness. Alan does. In the torchlight an Arab man can be seen running. His jacket looks stuffed with something.

Alan *WA-GIFF MEHALLAK!* [Stay where you are!]

Eddy and Grif turn to shine their torches on him too.

Eddy *INZIL!* [Get down!]

Grif *INZIL!* [Get down!]

Alan *WA-GIFF MAKENEK!* [Stop right there!]
INZIL 'AL-ARDH! [Get down on the floor!]

The Arab man ignores them, tries to scurry away.
A hail of gunfire brings him down.
Alan shines his torch on the corpse. He approaches it with great caution, pokes it with his gun. Alan gets down and listens to the jacket. He suddenly springs up and moves away from the corpse.

It's fizzing. Get back.

Eddy gets back, Grif has now joined him with his torch. They wait for a while. Before approaching again.

Grif If it's fizzing it means something's gone wrong. The fuse hasn't lit.

Alan approaches with Eddy, who shines the torch while Alan delicately undoes the jacket. Cans of Coke and Pepsi fall out. Some have been grazed by the bullets and are spraying cola out at angles.

Alan Ah shit. Ah Christ.

Alan slumps down, really upset. Grif approaches.

Was I was I the only one who engaged him, it was me, it was just me?

Eddy Would it feel better if it was me too?

Alan No. Maybe.

Grif The guy knew what he was doin. He heard you. He didn't listen.

Eddy It was me too.

Alan Was it?

Eddy (*beat*) No.
Go n' take a breather, pal.

Alan walks away disconsolate.

Alan FUCK!

Eddy and Grif look at each other.

Eddy Give him a minute, eh.

Grif nods. They look at the corpse.

You think he heard us?

Grif He heard us alright. Must be stolen.
I don't see you telling Al to stay calm.

Eddy picks up a can. He sucks some cola from one of the spraying Coke cans. Picks up one of the Pepsi cans.

Eddy What d'you prefer, Coke or Pepsi?

Grif Don't really give a damn, long as there's bourbon in it.

Eddy Here, take the taste test.

Grif is amused.

Well, close your eyes.

Grif does so. Under torchlight, Eddy hands one to him, with his thumb over the spraying hole. Grif sucks from it. Then he does the same with another can.

Grif I think. I think maybe the first one. Uhh. Yeah. The first one. It's kinda more. I dunno. I just like it better.

Eddy That's interesting. I said Coke. You said Pepsi.

Grif (*beat*) Let's call the whole thing off.

Eddy looks at the corpse.

Eddy Poor bastard. Shitty state of affairs dying for blackmarket soft drinks.

Eddy kneels down and pats the body's head, with great tenderness.

Sorry, pal.

Eddy and Grif swiftly drag the body away.

Act Two

ONE: THE ADHAN

The cast can be heard singing the Adhan, the morning call to prayer.

During the scene, Alan changes into a smart linen shirt and chinos. He tries to suppress a powerful yawn; he's exhausted.

The people Alan talks to are in different places with him:

Masha is outside the Russian bar she works in. She is carrying a toy helicopter in a box. Alan has surprised her.

Saad is on the landing of their hotel. He is on his hands and knees.

Eddy is in a bar with Alan; they have just attended Grif's memorial.

The Adhan overlaps briefly with the start of the exchanges.

Masha *Chyrt!* [Shit!] You again!

Alan I need to talk to you. About my friend.

Masha You wait for me? All night.

Alan You're the last person who saw Eddy after me.

Masha He not come back?

Alan No. He not come back.

Masha You wait all night? I tell you everything before.

Alan So you haven't seen him.

Saad turns from all fours to see Alan.

Saad Alan. It is very early.

Alan Oh, sorry to interrupt.

Saad No, is okay.

Alan Don't stop on my account.

Saad Come in. You're welcam.

Alan I'll go, let you pray.

Saad No, I am not praying now. I lose my key.

Saad holds up a very small key. Alan laughs.

Masha No, I'm sorry. Now please, I must go home.

Alan He hasn't been in your bar once?

Masha No!

Saad I am Muslim, but I do not pray always and. Do all of everything.

Masha You want I call security?

Saad You go to look for your friend tonight?

Alan Yeah, I talked to the girl who last saw him.

Masha looks at a printed picture of Eddy.

Saad You give out the page we make?

Alan Yeah, the Arabic helped a lot. Thank you.

Masha (*sighs*) Okay, I take.

Saad Welcam.
　　You think about your friend many times, I think.

Eddy You know what I'd like when we're outta this job. Cheeky wee beach bar. Spain, maybe.

Masha But I not see him.

Alan Could you put some up in the bar, where the girls change or something.

Saad Your friend, the lost one. He never tell you he is leave?

Eddy Always thought. An' I used to think I could run it wi' Claire, but. She wasn't the type to throw herself intay something like that.

Masha (*leaving*) Okay. Goodnight.

Alan (*points*) I like the Chinook. Who's it for?

Masha clutches the toy closely to her.

Masha (*defensively*) It is for friend. Child of a friend.

Saad I have a friend, in the Rifles, from Rother-ham. He say, 'Don't pull my pisser!'

Alan Good advice.

Saad It is a joke about his penis.

Masha It is called chopper, no?

Alan It's a Chinook because it has twin rotors. It has two – (*He gestures rotors, rather absurdly.*)

Saad You have no sleep? For the conference. Andre fly to Amman today.

Masha How you say?

Alan Shi-nuk.

Saad She like you. Carolyn. She ask many question about you.

Eddy Ay, you, me n' Grif coulda run a fine wee fuckin bar, couldn't we?

Masha Tell me about shi-nuk. So I can say. For the boy.

Alan Looks like an old model. Vietnam era. Chinook means very strong wind.

Saad She ask if you work hard.

Alan And you said?

Eddy For starters, wouldn'ta needed any security to speak of.

Saad I say, 'Hardest worker I ever see.'

Masha You stop your job?

Eddy Y'know, if there was a highlights package of your life, the job would be in it.

Masha No more Iraq money for you.

Alan It's not Iraqi money.

Masha Not any more!

Eddy The job would be most of it.

Saad You go to many places in Amman.

Alan I saw the refugee camps outside the city.

Eddy But there'll still come a day when I say, not doin this any more. Buy the bar and go.

Masha It's okay, I am same as you.

Alan What, cos you take Iraqi money?

Eddy Cut n' run.

Saad Million refugees in Jordan.

Masha I take American money, Jordanian, Egyptian, European. But all funeral business.

Alan All your customers are undertakers?

Saad Million in Syria, I think.

Masha When a person die, many people make money.

Eddy Not convinced about bein back home, ay.

Masha When a country die, also many people make money.

Eddy Home's a strange word for it.

Masha Cannot escape funeral business.

Alan But you could escape all this.

Saad I am lucky.

Masha Amman is escape. From Irkutsk.

Eddy You're like me, ay.

Saad Very lucky.

Eddy You don't feel at home any more even when you're at home.

Saad You can make two hours sleep I think, before conference. Sleep well.

They disperse.

TWO: PROFESSIONAL BUT STRIKING

We're in the company office/business suite in Amman. Harry is briefing Alan.

Harry Naturally, the people who want a man like Andre dead are those who want to strike a blow against the private military companies in Iraq, and to a lesser extent Afghanistan. For these people, Andre is a high-profile figure, okay, by virtue of his media, uh, profile that he has, okay?

Alan Sure.

Harry So it's extremists. I don't think this is any different to the sort of work you've found yourself doing in the past, but in Amman, of course, everything is less regimented.

Carolyn enters, quietly. She has some shirts on hangers.
They immediately look to her.

Carolyn Don't mind me.

They continue the briefing while Carolyn listens.

Harry It's really a one-man job here. Any more's gonna make him more of a target.

Alan No. Of course.

Harry Once you're in the conference itself, their security takes over, you go and do your conference job.

Carolyn Unless there's an emergency.

Harry Yes, unless there's an emergency, in which case, uh.

He looks at Carolyn.

Carolyn Find Andre, keep him covered.

Harry And don't worry if he's grouchy with you. He's very used to Paul, they've known each other a long time. He's pretty cheesed off cos Paul had to go and scoop up someone else's shit in Bangdad.

Carolyn looks pointedly at Alan.

Alan (*beat*) And I'll get introduced soon?

Harry Oh. You've never met him? (*To Carolyn.*) Alan's gonna meet Andre now, right.

Carolyn At the airport. Yes.

Harry How's his knee?

Carolyn He's had worse.

Harry You're telling me.

Carolyn Course, you know all about that.
Alright, Harry. Thanks.

Harry shakes Alan's hand and goes.

And how are you this morning?

Alan I don't think I'm cut out to be a salesman.

Carolyn You're a spokesperson.

Alan And I'm combining it with bein bodyguard to the world's most famous mercenary.

Carolyn He's a pussy cat. It's me you wanna watch.

Alan I am, don't worry.

They look at each other.

Carolyn Looking forward to it?

Alan I don't know what to expect really.

Carolyn Expect to be surprised. At the words you won't hear. And expect not to recognise the Iraq they talk about. And ignore that. Expect people making speeches, holding talks, giving gifts from pens to cars, shaking hands endlessly. And after it, expect us to come out with an increased market share. If things go well.

Alan And if things don't go well?

Carolyn Expect to come out with a lot of pens. (*Hands him folded paper.*) Do not forget this. It's Andre's opening speech. You're meeting him at the airport.

Alan Yeah, aren't you?

Carolyn No, I've got a hundred things to do here. And we see quite enough of each other as it is. D'you have an eye for a shirt?

She holds up one of her shirts on a hanger or in the dry cleaner's plastic.

Alan I've been reliably informed: no.

Carolyn Just tell me which looks better to you. As a man. Men being the main constituency one deals with at these events.

She finds another shirt.

I want professional but striking.

Completely without ceremony, she starts taking off her blouse. Alan turns around.

How are you going to tell me if you're not looking?

Alan You're getting changed.

She throws the blouse at him.

Carolyn Alan, hold that. And stop being embarrassed.

Alan I'm not embarrassed.

Carolyn Well, neither am I, so turn around.

He turns around.

Or should I be? Is that what you're saying?

Alan No.

Carolyn Do I have anything to be embarrassed about?

Alan No. Not at all.

Carolyn Well then.

She is holding the new shirt, undoing the buttons to put it on.

It occurs to me that you need to diversify.

Alan Meaning?

Carolyn Let's face it, your days of deploying are over. Your nerves are shot and your decision-making ability under pressure is extremely dubious.

Alan That's. Not fair.

Her phone rings.

Carolyn Bring that over here, will you.

He does. He shows her who it is. She gestures to him to hold the phone by her ear.

(*Into phone.*) Hello, Malcolm, yes, Andre got your email, Andre and I would be delighted to have lunch with you. I know, he's very excited about your ideas. Well, that's great. Listen, I must go. Give my love to – your wife. Bye Malcolm.

Nods at Alan to end the call.

Forgot his fucking wife's name.
Take this crucifix off, will you. Doesn't play all that well with some of the clients.

Alan fiddles with her crucifix. She is still undoing buttons.

Alan Good Christian girl?

Carolyn No. It was my father's.

Alan is having trouble with the crucifix.

Sometimes it helps to take something, after a death.

Full silence.

He went round the world with his battalion, spent the entirety of my childhood on the IRA hit. Then one day he goes swimming, has a stroke and drowns. It's funny, in its way.

Alan has taken the crucifix off. Carolyn is putting her shirt on.

Alan Least the IRA didn't get him.

Carolyn Aren't you the king of clutching at straws?
You'd make a good full-time rep. You have a trustworthy, capable demeanour.

Alan Thank you.

Carolyn As I know, of course, you're not all that trustworthy. But you *seem* so infallible.

Alan (*beat*) I'd be better off in Baghdad.

Carolyn is standing close to him, looking straight at him, perhaps doing her earrings.

Carolyn *Nobody* is better off in Baghdad. What time is it?

Alan Twenty past eight.

Carolyn You've probably got time to kiss me, but after that you *will* need to pick my husband up from the airport.

Full silence. Alan is sorely tempted.

Alan Can I be honest with you?
I really need to know where Eddy is.
I had to tell his poor fuckin mum.
She didn't even know he was missing.
I thought she'd have heard. From you or someone.
I need to stop doin this and go look for him properly.

Full silence.

Carolyn If you really wanted to find him you wouldn't be here.
How hard have you really looked?
It's not exactly a manhunt, is it?

Alan is hurt and about to leave.

Do you think people haven't done this before?
We offered you both compassionate leave. You both declined. Don't think I don't have sympathy. But ask yourself. How much sympathy can I *afford* to have?

People malfunction. In this industry. One of the few advantages I have is that I can see it early. Why do you think I don't let Andre deploy any more?

Now if you were to consider this role on a long-term basis, you can imagine the sort of perks you'd get.

Do the right thing. (*Kisses his cheek.*)

She leaves.

THREE: THE CONFERENCE

We hear background applause, garbled announcements in Arabic and English. Conference Exhibitors A, B and C welcome the audience with almost evangelical fervour. Their pitches can be spoken concurrently.

Exhibitor A Welcome to Project Rebuild Iraq!

Exhibitor B Welcome to the Near East. Thanks in part to our modern infrastructure and wide array of first-class hotels – billions of investment dollars are pouring in from around the world.

Exhibitor C Even in these difficult times for investors, Iraq's reconstruction market refuses to be anything less than robust.

Exhibitor A We're looking for people with vision. People with the vision to ignore the economic doom mongers and seize unique investment opportunities in the Near East.

Exhibitor B Entrepreneurship and ethical considerations go hand in hand at Project Rebuild Iraq.

Exhibitor A Welcome.

Exhibitor C Anyone not active in Iraq's reconstruction market simply must talk investment with us. We are creating a portfolio of the most lucrative and beneficial potential investments for our clients.

Exhibitor B From our point of view, this is *the* high-profile event of the year. We are showcasing the most ambitious, investment-opportunity-laden reconstruction undertakings of your era.

Exhibitor A Welcome.

Exhibitor C Welcome to Rebuild Iraq.

Exhibitor A Welcome to Jordan, the jewel of the Near East.

Exhibitor B During a necessary financial correction, fresh markets like Iraq are gold dust. Iraq's reconstruction market is worth tens of billions of dollars.

Alan is a bit lost amidst the noise and bustle. Sally sees him and approaches.

Sally Hey, it's Mister Merc with no Manners. Wow. I was right. (*Looks at his badge.*) PMC. You gotta story for me yet?

Alan Once upon a time, a girl from Reuters met a rude man. The rude man woke up the next day and was sorry.

Sally Did your friend show up?

Alan No. I've no idea where he is.

Sally What company are you? (*Looks at his badge.*) I'll come see you later.

Alan goes to his pocket for a pen or his phone, but Sally breezes past him. In his pocket he finds the speech Carolyn gave him. He runs to find Andre. Hands it to him. Andre looks at it.

Andre About time.

Alan Good luck. With your speech.

Andre looks witheringly at him.

Andre You should probably be manning the exhibit, eh?

During this exchange, Harry has stepped up to a lectern and has been giving a speech which Alan now watches from behind.

Harry We're a UK-based company, providing practical site-risk management consultancy, supported by tested security solutions. Whether yours is an effective low-profile solution or a high-profile deterrent, we can effectively address the threat while considering your business needs throughout. Our determination to provide the highest quality of service available is displayed with our can-do approach. Our strength is drawn from many years of operational service within highly testing environments. We pride ourselves on our client-led solutions, designed to be cost-effective and sustainable. All activities are conducted with the highest degree of discretion and integrity whilst at the same time maintaining complete transparency. We're committed to strict industry accountability and regulation. It is our ability to produce results in difficult environments that sets us apart. We provide experience, reliability and total professionalism to the challenge of modern conflict security. Our exhibit will be open for the duration. I'd be only too happy to personally explain more of what we offer.

Thank you for listening.

As Harry is speaking, Saad finds Alan. Saad is breathless.

Saad Alan! There is news.

Alan Uh-huh.

Saad It is bad, I think. Bad news.

Alan Okay.

Saad Your friend.

Alan Eddy?

Carolyn enters. She's been running.

Saad Yes.

Carolyn Saad. Are you –

She stares at Saad.

Alan WHAT?

Carolyn Saad. I'll tell him.

Alan Tell me what?

Saad Okay.

Carolyn looks at Saad, until he reluctantly leaves.

Alan Tell me what!

Carolyn There's someone who might be Ed Wallace. On an Islamist website. Hostage. They say he's a Scot. We've checked, we cannot positively identify him.

Alan Be straight with me. It looks like him?

Carolyn The sound and visual quality is extremely poor. If it's him. Then. Then we'll get him back. We'll do everything. Everything in our powers, I promise. And I apologise for what I said earlier.

Alan holds his stomach.

Alan What group are claiming to have him?

Carolyn We don't know.

Alan Sunni? Shia? They're in Iraq or in Jordan?

Carolyn We don't know anything. Not a thing.

She goes to subtly console him.

Please.

Alan pushes her away.

Alan Are you. Are you cracked? Andre's here somewhere.

Carolyn Go, back to the hotel. You can't be working now. But I don't think it's him.

Alan You weren't gonna tell me until after the job's done. (*Pointedly.*) I'll be manning the exhibit. I wouldn't want to let you guys down.

FOUR: PUBLIC RELATIONS

On the floor of the conference, an exchange is taking place between Alan and an Arab businessman in a headdress.
  Saad is translating.

Saad He says, it is important that the contractor not offend the citizens of Iraq. He says he does not trust American company and why he is interest in this British company.

  Alan is doing his best to be in charming, confident spokesman mode.

Alan That's great. Of course, the American companies are often bigger than us, with more money, but we feel we have more understanding of the street.

  Saad translates this, the man in the headdress nods and replies.
  It is a very courteous exchange.
  Even though he's nodding and maintaining eye contact with the businessman, there's still something slightly wild about Alan.

Saad Do you have enough money then to have best equipment for the company?

73

Alan Honestly, I've never had any problems with the equipment. I. I have to say. Although. No, no, problems come more from bad luck, normally.

Saad translates, then the man replies to Saad. Saad translates. Throughout this, Alan is straining to keep it together.

Saad And the men of the company, they are professional?

Alan Oh yes. Yeah, absolutely. Well, we're paid, aren't we.

Saad looks worriedly at Alan. The man in the headdress talks to Saad.

Saad Have you found the problems of Iraq to be improve?

Alan (*beat*) Well, Saad, why don't you tell him. You know better than I do.

Saad He is asking you.

Alan shrugs.

Alan Have the problems of Iraq improved?

Saad In your experience.

Alan What about your experience?

Saad He is *asking you.*

Alan What do I think about the problems of Iraq? (*Deadpan.*) I think that if you put your hand in a cow's arse and you pull. You pull what you think's the calf. And it's the guts, but you can't leave the calf in there so you keep pulling.

Saad Little slower, Alan.

Alan Then the cow hasn't got any guts left and the calf's prob'ly dead, but it's an honest mistake. But nobody really cares how honest the mistake is, cos there's cowshit and blood everywhere. So I think the obvious answer is, don't be a vet.

Saad's smile is strained. He starts translating back to the Businessman, obviously something other than what Alan has said. He turns back and is stern with Alan while sounding ostensibly courteous.

Saad Alan, don't talk about cows, talk about this company. He ask about contractors like you, if you go to Iraq because you want to help – say yes, he speaks some English.

Alan This guy's a regular Jeremy Paxman.

Saad is looking at Alan desperately.

Yes. (*Nods.*) I went cos it's better goin for money than for a bunch of ungrateful swine who think, once you're in a body bag, that you asked for it by joining up.

Saad starts to translate to the Businessman, it is still courteous. It becomes clear to the audience – through body language and other reactions – that Saad is not translating a word of what Alan is saying.

We think we're the good guys though. The good guys in all of this. And maybe we are, I've got no idea. Nobody has. If I was Iraqi I'd prob'ly fight every white bastard I saw. My best mate's got himself kidnapped, but before that a man I knew well for seven years was burned alive in front of me. Lad of twelve's blown him up with a Molotov cocktail. We killed the boy, obviously. But I've got no idea how he even got near us. Might've been my fault, the principal's fault, you could blame the company or even Grif himself. Or even just piss poor luck.

Saad Alan, please.

Saad is still pretending to translate, conducting a conversation with the man in the headdress. It is

completely incongruous with what Alan is saying.
Possibly Saad's Arabic is punctuated by English words
Alan hasn't used.

Alan So even though I knew Grif well, I didn't know him
that well, obviously, cos he –

Saad Alan, you are upset.

Alan Grif would regularly – Saad, translate this. Grif was
a great guy once. But he basically learned to trust nobody.
'Cept us. So he'd fire, just fire into crowds sometimes.
Not soldiers, civilians. And Grif told us he saw an RPG.
Or they had guns in the crowd. Don't think there ever
were. But I don't know, y'see.

Saad stops translating, aghast.

Saad This is true?

Alan You're not translating.

Saad looks at Alan, hurt. Then turns, smiles as best he
can and continues translating.

Saad, tell him honestly: we're pretty good.
    Tell him we're much better than every other fucker out
there. Cos for every guy like Eddy, for every guy tryin to
be a pro, there's a psychopath. And for every psychopath,
there's a cowboy. And they're actually more dangerous
than a psychopath. Cos where a psychopath might pick
off a couple of locals just for kicks, a cowboy's liable to
kill everybody in a twenty-metre radius – including him
and you – completely through his own fuckin stupidity.
And his shitty training.

Possibly the Businessman has already departed and
Alan is now railing with no focus.

And we don't have any cowboys on our staff, we're
mostly pros and psychopaths. So tell him, Saad, tell him
we're the guys for him. Tell him we're –

An alarm sounds. The same alarm as at the start of the play.

Pandemonium. The same announcements. Alan looks around.

Alan Where's Andre?

Saad He is giving his speech.

Alan sprints away.

FIVE: TOTAL GANGFUCK

Grif, Alan and Eddy are in the armoured vehicle, as in Act One, Scene Three. Alan should still be in his conference garb of shirt and chinos. The men have just registered they're alive after the I.E.D. scare.

Alan Was that a fuckin Big Mac wrapper?

Silence.

Grif I think it was a Whopper.

Eddy Was that. Some prize cunt's dropped a Whopper box in the middle / of the road!

Grif Jesus Christ, why didn't we see that earlier.

Alan I don't think Whoppers come in boxes.

Eddy Let's decide what the fuck it was later –

Grif I think they do, they – CLEAR?

Eddy ALL CLEAR.

Grif I think they come in, no! No, / they come in that –

Alan Whoppers come in that silvery –

Grif – silvery, yeah, / paper.

Eddy Keep your HEADS ON. I don't wanna be talking about fuckin hamburgers.

Alan Whoa whoa, he's slowin up.

Grif (*in rear-view mirror*) What the fuck's he doin?

Alan is frantically waving at the truck to keep moving. Car horns can be heard, one of them Grif's.

Alan (*gesturing*) Keep movin, y' bastard!

Eddy What sort of a total gangfuck does this look like?

Grif Think it's a come-on?
You told 'im, don't fuckin stop whatever 'appens.

Eddy You heard me.

Grif Well then, he's on the mudjahadeen payroll and we're leavin 'im.

Grif goes to drive off.

Alan He's goin fuckin wild waving at us. Think he's pointing at the dashboard.

Grif I don't trust it.

Alan What's the S.O.P. here?

Eddy The S.O.P. is call the cunt up on the comms n' ask him why he's tryna get us all murdered.

Grif Right, we're leavin him. (*Goes to drive off.*)

Eddy But we don't have any comms, so I'll go n' ask him myself, how's that?

Grif We're fuckin leavin 'im, Eddy!

Eddy has ducked out of the vehicle.

Grif Fuckin hell, Eddy. This is bullshit! This has got trap written all over it.

Alan The driver's as confused as we are. What can you see?

Grif Coupla kids playing with sticks. Waitin for the Al-Quaeda cavalry comin over the horizon, no doubt.

There is the crackle of a voice on his radio.

(*On radio.*) Roger that, Tommo. Eddy's out there now, being a fuckin hero.

Alan is watching the horizon.

Eddy (*on radio*) He's runnin on empty.

Alan It's petrol, fucker needs petrol.

Grif How the fuck's he run out of petrol?

Alan Maybe bullet to the tank, I dunno.

Grif That's bollocks, it's a fuckin trap.

Alan No, Eddy can see the fuel gauge.

Grif Doesn't mean it's not a trap, leave the driver and we'll get outta here.

Alan We leave that cargo, we might as well sack the whole rotation in.

Grif We need to get movin. Eddy'll get that sorted, they'll get fuel from the other lot.

Alan (*beat*) Leave 'em?

Grif We're gonna get fucking roasted out here.

Alan Leave those poor fucks on Route Irish?

Grif We're sittin askin to be fucking killed out here.

Alan Eddie too. Grif? Grif, Eddie too.

Grif Look, fuck, I dunno what I'm saying.

Alan (*beat*) I'll take him our petrol, we'll be quicker.

Grif Don't you get out as fuckin well. I'm askin to get killed sittin here.

Alan has gone.

Al!

Al!

Fuck you, Al! Fuck's sake.

Grif is now alone. He scans the horizon and his rear-view mirror. He anxiously hums to himself, the tune of 'Bread of Heaven'.

He's about to start the vehicle when he sees something to his left, in the audience. He looks at it intently. Then fear rises in him suddenly and he's just about to burst out of his seat when the lights go out on him.

SIX: THE SCARE

Andre and Alan are in a designated Emergency Area, located in one of the conference building's concrete back corridors. Alan is in bodyguard mode, so has a handgun on his person, in a holster or tucked into the back of his belt.

Alan This is us, Andre.

Andre Why here?

Alan Each exhibit has an emergency area. This is ours.

Andre Delightful.

They wait. Alan is recovering, subdued, a little awkward in Andre's presence.

Silence.

Andre So it's your first day as my PSD. And you knock me over two days after knee surgery. For what? A siren. Great start.

Alan I apologise again. (*Beat.*) Just instinct, I s'pose. (*Beat.*) How did your speech go? Up to that point.

Andre Well enough. (*Beat.*) And it wasn't my speech. I didn't write it.

Silence.

These conferences are just circuses. Bullshit circuses.
Necessary evil. Do you want a cigarette?

Alan (*beat*) Yeah. No. Thanks.

Andre lights a cigarette.

Andre Do something for me, friend.

Alan Sure.

Andre I've seen you n' my wife.

Alan (*beat*) Yeah.

Andre You like to talk, eh?

Alan She's my employer.

Full silence.

Andre No need to mention – (*Indicates the cigarette.*)

Alan No problem.

Andre smokes.

Andre This bomb scare's a godsend.
I should be laid up in bed.

Alan What happened to your leg?

Andre Just. Sports injury.

Alan Oh right. What – (*Beat.*) What sport?

Andre (*beat*) I play a lotta sports. I used to play a lot more, eh. Use your body while you can, that's my advice.
What they ask you today?

Alan On the floor?

Andre Yeah.

Alan They asked me about relations with Iraqis.

Andre Of course they did. With the government licences now, it's all we're ever asked. One day I'll say 'Friend. There are no good relations in this war. Because we can't drink with them. And we can't fuck them.'

Alan That's not the only reason though, is it?

Andre You don't win hearts and minds. You win stomachs. You win dicks and livers and cunts.
    Look at Vietnam. Guys came out of there with wives, lifelong friends. None of that here. There's a few Iraqis: they like wine, like democracy, the good things in life. Where the fuck are they? They're here. They're in Jordan. Of course they're in Jordan. They're not bloody fools.
    But then, the truth has no place at the circus.

Alan First casualty of war. (*Beat.*) That's what they say, isn't it?

Andre Truth is the first casualty of thinking too much. (*Stubs his cigarette.*) All we have, in this conflict, is the gift of our professionalism.
    We have one long-lasting legacy to this region. Companies like ours. Who will provide an umbrella, under which Iraq can rebuild itself.
    It's important we do this right. It's a life's work. Long after troops have left, we will remain.
    It won't be real. The scare. Just trying to disrupt us.

Alan Carolyn rang me three times, but with the alarm going off I missed the calls. And we're out of network here. What d'you reckon?

Andre (*beat*) Go and find her.

Alan Yeah?

Andre Ya. Of course. Might be important.

Alan Alright.

Alan exits.
Andre waits around. He's alone, and relaxes. He untangles some white headphones and puts them in his ear. He's listening to music.
He plays some badminton shots with his walking stick.
Eddy enters, slowly. He is dishevelled. Andre can't hear him.

Eddy Sorry, are you Andre Classens?

Andre (*pulling the headphones out*) Hmm? Sorry, one second.

Eddy Andre Classens, right?

Andre Ya, that I am. Have we met?

Eddy No, no, we haven't, but I've heard of you, of course. Could you autograph this?

Eddy hands him a copy of Soldier of Fortune *magazine.*

Andre You at the conference?

Eddy No. No, I'm not.

Andre is signing the magazine.

Andre But you work for a PMC.

Eddy Aye, used to.

Andre Which one?

Eddy (*beat*) Your one.

Full silence. Andre studies him.

Andre And what happened?

Eddy produces a handgun. He's not nervous, but not in total control. Andre calms himself and stands upright, staring Eddy down. He holds the magazine out.

Do you want your magazine back?

Eddy Throw it down n' come this way till you cannae be seen.

Andre limps nearer him.

Don't come too close.

Andre You're on camera.

Eddy No I'm not.

Andre (*beat*) This is planned then.

Eddy just looks at him.

The bomb scare.

Eddy nods once. Andre takes a deep breath, rests on his stick.

Eddy What happened to your leg?

Andre (*beat*) Sports injury.

Eddy What were you doin?

Andre Just –
A racket sport. It's not important.
Let me live, and this is the end of it.
I give you my word.

Eddy just looks at him.

Alright. Why?

Eddy Your firm. That I trusted. That I was proud of. Left us to do our work. Without the necessary equipment. You. Did not uphold. Your end. Of the bargain.

Andre No deployment is ever perfect.

84

Eddy We had no radio contact with our principal.

Andre You want to shoot me for this.

Eddy And my pal was killed cos of that. There's a way to do things. Mister Classens. You bring people out here on straitjacket contracts. And you let them down so hard.

Eddy raises the gun higher, girding himself on.
Andre fixes him in a stare.

Andre Listen.
Your friends die.
I know how it is.

Eddy Do you?

Andre I've had it. Many times.
Found one man, a Zulu man. His face hanging off.
Two kids, they took turns on him with machetes.
That man stopped me drowning, a year before.
As I buried him, he moved his neck.
He was blinded. Bones loose in his flesh.
I shot him. Then I buried him.
Now I blamed every bastard I could.
But his death was his own.
It was a fool moment.
We have fool moments.
This is a fool moment.
Bring the gun down.
What's your name?
This is / how it is.

Eddy Don't pull this fuckin Afrikaan man of the jungle shit on me.

Andre A great man once said, 'When you have to kill, it costs nothing to be polite.'

Eddy That so?

Andre Great British man said that.

Eddy Who?

Andre He was prime minister.

Eddy Tell me who it was!

Andre Mid-twentieth century British / prime minister.

Eddy This isn't *Give Us a* fuckin *Clue*!

Alan enters. Eddy sees him first.

AL!

Alan freezes, staring at Eddy.

Alan Wh – Eddy. (*Relief.*) I thought you were kidnapped.

Andre You know this man?

Eddy (*his gun still up*) Why aren't you in Iraq?

*Alan wanders into the path of the gun, between Andre
and Eddy.*

Alan Cos of you.

Eddy Move, Al!

Andre Do. Your. Job.

Alan You didn't check your emails. What're you –

Eddy FUCKIN MOVE, AL!

Alan Put the gun down – I'm just glad you're safe.

*Andre pulls out Alan's handgun and shoots Eddy in
the head, killing him.*
*Alan falls over. And screams. He throws himself on
Eddy's body.*

Andre You are employed for my security. And you just
stand there.

Alan He wasn't gonna kill you.

Andre You're sure about that? I've had a lot of guns
pointed at me.

He breathes deeply. Slumps down and sits. Alan is now numb with shock.

I'm fuckin retired, I don't need this.

Full silence.

He said a man died.

No response.

One of our men.

Alan weakly nods.

He said there were complications.
Because of the company.
Or the contractor?

*Alan looks at Andre. He might formulate some words.
He doesn't. Maybe he weakly shrugs.
   Saad enters and sees the body.
   Saad and Andre look at each other.*

Saad You are safe?

Andre nods.

Andre Where's my wife, Saad?

Saad She. She has gone back to hotel.

Andre I need you to tell the police. And the conference organisers. (*Points to Eddy.*) This man was shot in self-defence. (*Points at Alan.*) This man is a witness. (*Points to himself.*) This man will be at the hotel. Clear? (*To Alan.*) You almost let me die very cheaply, young man.
   Very fucking cheaply indeed.

Andre walks off.

Saad You are safe? What happen?

Full silence.

Who is that?

Alan That is Eddy.
  My friend.
  The lost one.

Alan breaks down in tears.
  Saad goes and hugs Alan. It is not histrionic. Just
  deeply felt.
  Christian organ music can be heard.

SEVEN: EDDY'S EULOGY

A chapel in Wales. The audience are attending a memorial
service.
  The Christian organ music continues. Hymn sheets are
passed round.
  Eddy comes to the lectern, with a pre-written speech.
He delivers the eulogy with controlled emotion.

Eddy We've heard about Christopher, the family man.
  And he was a fine family man.
  But I've been asked today to talk about the Christopher
that I knew.
  Christopher was known to me, and hundreds of
servicemen and women,
  Simply as Grif.
  Grif was so many things.
  Grif was a proud Welshman and a proud member of
the British Army.
  When we left the Parachute Regiment, Grif became a
proud security guard, doin the toughest job on earth, in
Baghdad.
  Grif was an excellent soldier who earned respect from
everyone he came into contact with.
  And Grif was my mate that I'll never forget.

Eddy looks over at Alan.

The day that he died, I was there.

I'm sorry to say that, but I'm happy also cos I can be sure how quick it was.

If I could of died bringin back his body, I woulda.

May sound dramatic, but it's true.

Alan gives him a burning look.

'N' I'm sorry to speak this way with family present, but it needs sayin. Things went terribly wrong that day. And I won't ever forget it.

But what Grif did won't just last for a few years. Or a decade. It'll last longer 'an 'at. Because that man, who many of you knew as Christopher, put his blood, and his heart, and his soul, and ultimately his life, aye, into the earth of Iraq. And as that country is bein rebuilt. With every new house and factory and office that goes up in that country, people should think of him. And be proud. Because that's history that he made. And you all knew him. 'N' you can be proud too.

Full silence.

We're gonna sing now. Christopher was a Welsh rugby fan to the end, he was always singin this song, the lyrics o' which amused him a wee bit, I seem to remember.

An organ starts up. The cast sing 'Bread of Heaven, by William Williams, from their service sheets.

All

Guide me, O thou great Redeemer
Pilgrim through this barren land

Eddy is busting his lungs singing, emotion swelling up in him.

Alan looks across at him.

I am weak but Thou art mighty
Hold me with Thy powerful hand.

Bread of Heaven! Bread of Heaven!
Feed me till I want no more
Feed me till I want no more.

Open now the crystal fountain
Whence the healing waters flow
Let the fiery, cloudy pillar
Lead me all my journey through.

The lights slowly begin to isolate Alan, but everyone is singing.

Strong Deliv'rer, Strong Deliv'rer
Be Thou still my strength and shield
Be Thou still my strength and shield.

The other voices die away. We can hear and see only Alan.

Alan
When I tread the verge of Jordan
Bid my anxious fears subside
Death of death, and hell's destruction,
Land me safe on Canaan's side.

Bread of Heaven! Bread of Heaven!
Feed me till I want no more
Feed me till I want no more.

Alan is completely isolated by light. He sings the final lines again. He is singing his heart out.

Feed me till I want no more
Feed me till I want no more.

Alan is standing still, his face registering traces of emotion.

Lights out on Alan.